Incentives in Community-based Health Insurance Schemes

T0316489

DEVELOPMENT ECONOMICS AND POLICY

Series edited by Franz Heidhues and Joachim von Braun

Vol. 43

PETER LANG

Frankfurt am Main · Berlin · Bern · Bruxelles · New York · Oxford · Wien

Incentives in Community-based Health Insurance Schemes

F. Markus Kaiser

PETER LANG

Europäischer Verlag der Wissenschaften

Bibliographic Information published by Die Deutsche Bibliothek
Die Deutsche Bibliothek lists this publication in the Deutsche Nationalbibliografie; detailed bibliographic data is available in the internet at <http://dnb.ddb.de>.

Zugl.: Bielefeld, Univ., Diss., 2003

D 361
ISSN 0948-1338
ISBN 3-631-52687-3
US-ISBN 0-8204-7315-4

© Peter Lang GmbH
Europäischer Verlag der Wissenschaften
Frankfurt am Main 2004
All rights reserved.

Printed in Germany 1 2 4 5 6 7

www.peterlang.de

To

Katinka & Jost

Preface

While health care systems in developed countries are becoming more expensive, increasing the financial burden for employees, employers and taxpayers, in developing countries coverage is usually poor and often not available. Most developed countries provide medical care through compulsory or tax financed health care systems. In contrast, less developed countries are not able to apply these tools nationwide due to a lack of enforcement capacity and/or financial resources. Instead, community-based health insurance schemes (CBHI) try to fill the gap and provide reasonable medical care. CBHI are based on voluntarism, meaning that participation is determined by factors such as health status and income. These factors limit or support the growth of CBHI. The question therefore is: How can the limiting factors be overcome to increase the coverage rate of CBHI.

The following work of F. Markus Kaiser suggests an innovative and unconventional approach to boost membership figures and coverage rates of CBHI. A key problem of CBHI is that authorities cannot sanction non-members. Membership cannot be enforced. The author thus proposes to award membership by offering non-health related incentives for joining a CBHI. He designed a raffle model within the CBHI, which entitles everyone joining the CBHI to participate in a raffle game. This approach can attract new CBHI members and can be a motivation to continue membership payments of healthy insurance members, even if they receive no or less benefits from the insurance than those who use medical care. To assess whether the raffle approach could be successful, F. Markus Kaiser conducted an ex-ante demand analysis in Guimaras, a province in the Philippines. The results are promising. The majority (88.5 percent) of the members of an existing CBHI would like to participate in the raffle, while for 81.4 percent of current non-members a raffle would provide an incentive to join the CBHI. The respondents would even agree to higher premium payments of 50 percent to cover costs for administration and awards to run that raffle.

A one-to-one adoption of conventional health care financing tools will not be realizable in most developing countries. Therefore, innovative approaches are required to meet local requirements and cultural preconditions. The following raffle approach appears to be one promising tool to increase the coverage rate of CBHI and access to medical care for poor population groups.

Prof. Dr. Franz Heidhues   Prof. Dr. Joachim von Braun
Center for Tropical Agriculture   International Food Policy Research Institute
University of Hohenheim   (IFPRI) Washington D.C.

Acknowledgements

Many people were involved in this study and without their help and fruitful comments, it could not have been undertaken. I am particularly indebted to my supervisor, Prof. Dr. Ulrich Laaser, University of Bielefeld, Germany, who provided me with excellent intellectual and academic guidance and always found time to answer my questions. My second adviser, Prof. Dr. Beatrice Knerr, University of Kassel, Germany, gave me instructive inputs, particularly on poverty issues, and helped me widen my horizon. Both of them took very good care of me.

The field research was conducted in the Philippines, where Anne Nicolay, Project Coordinator GTZ, Philippines, opened the doors to decision makers in the Department of Health, the Philippine Health Insurance and the Guimaras Health Insurance Project. She and Chito Novales organized my stay in the Philippines, and shared their insights to the various peculiarities of the local community. I would also like to thank for the financial and technical support given to me by GTZ. During the field research, five research assistants helped me in conducting the interviews. They were Gilda Gepilano, Maricon Quidato, Karren Joy Gabasa, Nena Ganchillas and Luis Tronco Jr.

Special thanks go to Dr. Johannes Jütting, OECD, France, who encouraged me to write this Ph.D thesis and to Ronald Mangubat, Philippines, who helped me edit the final manuscript. Finally, I would like to thank my wife who was with me in the entire process. With her sound and helpful comments, she made a significant contribution to this study. All remaining errors are my sole responsibility.

F. Markus Kaiser

March 2004, Shanhua, Taiwan

Preface	7
Acknowledgements	9
Contents	11
Tables	13
Figures	14
Acronyms and Abbreviations	15

1. Introduction 17

1.1. Problem Setting 17
1.2. Objective of the Study and Major Research Questions 18
1.3. Outline of the Study 19

2. Strategies to Cope with Risks in Rural Areas 20

2.1. Sources of Risk in Rural Areas 20
2.2. Players in Rural Risk Sharing 22
2.3. Individual Strategies on Household Level to Cope with Risk 23
    2.3.1. Marriage and Migration 24
    2.3.2. Networks Based on Ethnic Ties, Kinship, and Sex 24
    2.3.3. Diversification of Income Sources 24
    2.3.4. Informal Credit Arrangements and Gift Exchange 26
2.4. Micro-Finance Institutions and their Role in Rural Risk Sharing 27

3. The Role of Community-based Health Insurance in Rural Risk Sharing 34

3.1. Community Health Care Financing Mechanisms 34
3.2. The Chances and Limits of Community-based Health Insurance Schemes 37
3.3. Lessons Learned and Policy Implications 39

4. Incentives and Social Health Insurance – a Theoretical Approach 41

4.1. Decision under Risk and Uncertainty - Gambling and Insurance 41
4.2. Considerations to Contribute to Public Goods 48
4.3. Linking the Provision of Public Goods with Lotteries 51
4.4. Introducing Incentives in Social Health Insurance: The Raffle Model 53

5. Research Methodology   57

5.1. Sample Selection and Data Collection   57
5.2. Development of the Regulations for Increasing the
Value of the Lot   59

6. Socio-Economic Overview on the Philippines and the Province Guimaras   61

6.1. The Philippines at a Glance   61
6.2. Health Status in the Philippines   63
6.3. The Province of Guimaras   65
6.4. Health Status in Guimaras   66

7. The Guimaras Health Insurance Project   69

7.1. Financial Facts and Figures   69
7.2. The GHIP Benefits   72

8. Results   75

8.1. Analysis on the GHIP   75
8.1.1. Necessity for a Health Insurance on Guimaras   76
8.1.2. Necessity for an Improved Communication Strategy   78
8.1.3. GHIP's Contribution for Reducing Out-of-Pocket Spending 79
8.2. Willingness to Join the Raffle   80
8.3. Willingness to Pay for the Raffle   82
8.4. Determinants to Participate in the Raffle within the GHIP 86
8.4.1. Variables Influencing the Likelihood to Join the Raffle 86
8.4.2. Model 1: Determinants for Joining the Insurance:
Members and Non-Members   89
8.4.3. Model 2: Determinants for Joining the Raffle:
Members and Non-Members   90
8.4.4. Model 3: Determinants for Joining the Raffle:
Non-Members   91
8.4.5. Model 4: Determinants for Joining the Raffle:
Members   93

9. Summary and Conclusion   94

9.1. Summary of Main Findings   94
9.2. Lessons Learned and Policy Implications   96
9.3. Future Research Needs   97

10. References   99

Tables

Table 1: Main Sources of Risk   21
Table 2: Different Functions and Strategies of Microfinance   27
Table 3: Typology of Insurance Examples in Less-Developed Countries   31
Table 4: CBHI's Payment Mechanisms – Limits and Benefits   36
Table 5: Three-Stage-Model of Raffle Regulations Combined
        with a CBHI Scheme   55
Table 6: Population & Number of Households in the Selected Barangays   57
Table 7: Raffle Regulations for the GHIP   59
Table 8: Inequality on Consumption Based on 1997 Data   62
Table 9: Total Health Care Expenditure per Sector in 1999   64
Table 10: Ten Leading Causes of Mortality in the Philippines (1998)   64
Table 11: Population of Guimaras by Municipalities   65
Table 12: Morbidity, Leading Causes (2000)   67
Table 13: Mortality, Leading Causes (2000)   67
Table 14: Health Insurance Coverage on Guimaras   68
Table 15: GHIP Membership Statistics Based on GHIP Data   70
Table 16: GHIP Contributions   70
Table 17: GHIP Staff and Salaries   71
Table 18: GHIP Ceilings for Drug Reimbursement   72
Table 19: The GHIP Benefits   73
Table 20: Claims Statistics GHIP   73
Table 21: Household Income in Pesos   75
Table 22: Financing the Out –of-Pocket Payment   77
Table 23: The Financing of Illness and the Sum Paid Out-of-Pocket
         During the Last 12 Months   80
Table 24: Reasons for Joining the Raffle in the GHIP   81
Table 25: Most Important Problems   82
Table 26: Willingness to Pay for the Raffle   83
Table 27: Ordinal Regression: Willingness to Pay for the Raffle   85
Table 28: Overview of Variables Used with the Expected Outcome   88
Table 29: Determinants for Joining the GHIP:
         Members and Non-Members   89
Table 30: Determinants for Joining the Raffle:
         Members and Non-Members   90
Table 31: Determinants for Joining the Insurance and the Raffle:
         Non-Members   92
Table 32: Determinants for Joining the Insurance and the Raffle:
         Members   93

Figures

Figure 1: Potential for Insurance as a Coping Strategy 30
Figure 2: Hypothetical Value Function 45
Figure 3: Hypothetical Weighting Function 46
Figure 4: Model of a CBHI Combined with a Raffle 54
Figure 5: Sum Paid for Medical Care (Out of Pocket)
During the Last 12 Months 76
Figure 6: Affordability of Health Care Expenses in the Next Month 77
Figure 7: Time Needed to Afford the Treatment Again 78
Figure 8: Preferred Raffle Prizes 81

Acronyms and Abbreviations

ADB	Asian Development Bank
BHW	Barangay Health Worker
CBR	Crude Birth Rate
CDR	Crude Death Rate
CU	Currency Unit
FTSE	Full Time Staff Equivalent
GDP	Gross Domestic Product
GHIP	Guimaras Health Insurance Project
GTZ	Deutsche Gesellschaft für Technische Zusammenarbeit
HALE	Healthy Life Expectancy
HC	Health Care
IMR	Infant Mortality Rate
MFI	Micro-Finance Institutions
PPP	Purchasing Power Parity
RoSCAs	Rotating Saving and Credit Associations
SEWA	Self-Employed Women's Association
SRM	Social Risk Management
TB	Tuberculosis
UNDP	United Nations Development Programme
WHO	World Health Organization
WTP	Willingness to Pay

1. Introduction

1.1. Problem Setting

In developing countries, poor people are exposed to many types of risks. These include natural risks such as drought and flood, risks due to political instability or environmental risks. Another risk that affects in particular people employed by the informal sector is the lack of properly protection against the risks of illness. Health of poor people is in jeopardy, because of insufficient hygiene, missing knowledge or carelessness towards the risks of illness. Developing countries account for 93 percent of the worldwide burden of disease and 84 percent of world population, however, they account for only 18 percent of global income and 11 percent of global health spending (Schieber and Maeda, 1999). Despite considerable efforts on the part of policy-makers, development institutions and donor agencies, it is estimated that over 50 percent of the population in developing countries remains uncovered against basic risks (Jütting, 1999). While state-based medical treatment is offered in some developing countries, often they are not be accessible to those who need medical protection, due to either high user fees or unacceptable long travel distances. On the other hand, private safety nets often can not cope with the cost of illness. Therefore, out of pocket spending for medical care is common in poor countries. In sixty percent of countries at incomes below $1000 per capita, out of pocket payment is 40 percent (WHO, 2000), with the negative effect that the poorest people of the society are excluded from medical treatment and access is restricted to those, who can afford it. In contrast, prepayment guarantees a fair way to finance a health system due to spread the financial risk among the members of a pool.

> *"In developing countries, therefore, the objective is to create the conditions for revenue collecting mechanisms, that will increasingly allow for separation on contributions from utilization. ..., this means promoting job-based contribution systems where possible, and facilitating the creation of community or provider-based prepayment schemes"* (WHO, 2000, p. 98)

This suggestion by WHO calls for agencies with strong institutional and organizational capacity that can perform collecting activities. State-based systems often fail or are not able to provide adequate coverage due to high transaction costs. However, community-based health insurance schemes (CBHI) have been regarded by WHO as a possible solution to fill this gap. These schemes reduce the risks of illness of informal sector workers and have the ability to expand the health insurance membership alongside government revenue. Unfortunately, the poorest of the poor cannot be reached even by such schemes due to unaffordable contributions. Usually, the poorest households depend on of state - or NGO-financed welfare programs or traditional social security systems. Most of the

CBHI appeared to be targeted at the rural middle class. However, CBHI are regarded as a key instrument to strengthen the protection against the risks of illness in the informal sector. (Dror and Preker, 2001)

1.2. Objective of the Study and Major Research Questions

A major problem that CBHI suffer from is low coverage. Bennett et al. (1998) reviewed 82 health insurance schemes worldwide. Most of them reach less than 30 percent of the target group. Some schemes have tried to expand their coverage with marketing and information as well as education and communication campaigns to promote their benefit package. Simply assuming the product health insurance would be bought once available has not paid out. Once subscribed, many insurees are not satisfied with the package, because during the design phase, many CBHI ignore the importance of consumer satisfaction or even the needs of the target group. In consequence of the mistakes made earlier, many schemes have modified their regulations, benefits packages and communication strategies to boost consumer satisfaction and to attract new members (Bennett et al., 1998).

Most CBHI are highly dependent on government or NGO subsidies. This is not necessarily a problem as long as the governmental influence on the scheme's politics is low, but the degree of subsidies could be an indicator for the success of the design's scheme. Other problems that CBHI face can be summarized as followed (Wiesmann, Jütting, 2000)[1]:

- **Moral hazard** means the unnecessary use of medical treatment by insured people and their attitude to get an immediate benefit of their paid premium without respecting the idea of insurance.

- **Adverse selection** describes the problem that an insurance is most attractive to high risk than for low risk groups. Generally, the sustainability of CBHI depends on risk sharing. Often, "good risks" appear to discontinue their membership after a trial period, because they do not receive the benefits that sick people get (Supakankunti, 2001).

- **Covariant risks** arise in small groups, which are not widely spread geographically and when the majority of the insurance members is hit by a catastrophe at the same time. For example: Epidemic infections due to no access to clean water, deficiency disease due to crop failure or infections.

- **The containment of costs** is difficult to achieve. The paradox of health care demand is, however, that what is perfectly rational for the individual is not necessarily rational for the society or the group of insurees. This is because health care involves life-dead decisions or at least health-ill decisions (Bogg et al. 1995).

---

1   See f. e.: Bogg et al. (1995), Bennett et al. (1998), Atim (1999) or Stierle (2000).

This study analyses possible solutions to increase membership figures with the effect of improved risks sharing and cost containment. The assumption of this thesis is that an incentive like a raffle game within health insurance can stabilize or even increase membership figures, while simultaneously improving the risks profile due to offering participation in health education or vaccination programs. It is hypothesized that a raffle combined with CBHI provides healthy individuals an immediate benefit and membership becomes more attractive for uninsured "good risks" and improves the risk profile. Further, the raffle approach provides an additional incentive for participation and reduces the drop out rates.

The main research questions of this study are: Would an implementation of a positive incentive, i.e. a raffle game, raise membership figures and improve risk pooling and what are the determinants for participation in a suggested raffle game? How much would the target group be willing to pay for this additional incentive?

1.3 Outline of the Study

In chapter 2 we take a closer look on social risk management in rural areas in general and what strategies poor people apply to cope with risky situations. Traditional risk protection tools such as marriage and migration are discussed, as well as advanced approaches as credit, savings and insurance programs offered by microfinance institutions. In chapter 3, the chances and limits of CBHI in the context of the provision of protection against the risks of illness are discussed. The theoretical framework in chapter 4 focuses on decision and game theory, which helps to understand how individuals decide when they have to make decisions with high risks involved. Additionally, we analyze the circumstances under which individuals are willing to participate in the provision of a public good. Based on the findings of the decision and game theory a raffle model will be presented as a new approach to increase participation rates in CBHI.

The research methodology of this study in chapter 5 provides information on the sample selection, the data collection and development of the questionnaire followed by an overview in chapter 6 on socio-economic data of the Philippines and the province of Guimaras, where the study took place. In chapter 7 the results of the analysis of the Guimaras Health Insurance Project (GHIP) provide insight of the strength and weakness of the CBHI and how the raffle model could improve the performance. Finally, in chapter 8 the results of the study are presented based on a willingness to join and willingness to pay analysis for the raffle

2. Strategies to Cope with Risks in Rural Areas

Traditional systems of social security are often the sole backbone of risks sharing. Where no sufficient government assistance is provided, people cope with crop seasonality, calamity and physical illnesses by using family ties and a network of friends. Diversification of income sources also helps to overcome risky situations. Cases of food shortage can be avoided by stocking up with provisions, the adjustment of consumption, or the selling of livestock. However, these traditional strategies are often not sufficient to cope with more cost-intensive risks. At this point, microfinance institutions (MFI) can provide assistance in case of unforeseeable "shocks" or life-changing events such as funeral costs or marriage dowry.

Three main strategies, which can substitute traditional systems of social security against the risks of daily life, are savings, loans, and insurance. (Agarwal, 1991) This chapter focuses on financing mechanisms by providing saving accounts, granting loans or insuring people against low frequency but high-costs risks. Later in this chapter, we will take a closer look on what role, especially community-based health insurance schemes, play in rural risk sharing strategies. This section provides insight on how disadvantaged groups in rural areas manage their exposure to risk and what kind of instruments of risk protecting mechanisms they are using.

2.1. Sources of Risk in Rural Areas

Poor households living in rural areas bear a heavy burden of risks, causing direct welfare losses, which lead to inefficiencies. This further results in risks-dealing strategies, which concentrate on lower risk and lower return assets. Meanwhile those who are more privileged tend to be less risk-averse than the poor and thus suffer proportionally greater welfare losses for different levels of risks. (Morduch 1995, Jalan and Ravaillon 1998) The impact of a risk or the combination with other risks can be regarded as a function of frequency, intensity, duration, spread of the risk and the size of the effective risk pool. (Siegel and Alwang, 1999, p.7) The main sources of risk can be distinguished in covariant and idiosyncratic risks. Covariant risks affect many households simultaneously as drought, flood or communicable diseases, while idiosyncratic risk refers to household specific risk as non-communicable diseases or the loss of the breadwinner. "Risks" will therefore be defined as a phenomenon that refers to uncertain events and outcomes with known or unknown probabilities. (Siegel and Alwang, 1999)

The risks shown in table 1 affect the social conditions and the social status of a household. These factors are known to contribute to poverty. Generally, it can be differentiated between three strategies to reduce the shock of a risky event (Holzmann and Jørgensen, 2000). With *preventive strategies,* people try to lower the probability of an incident. Those strategies have a very large scope that surpasses the traditional area of social protection, which include policies in the area of macroeconomics, public health, education and environment protection. Another strategy to reduce the impact of the aftermath of a risky situation is the *mitigation strategy.* This strategy uses portfolio diversification, i.e. different assets, different crops and different kinds of animals or informal or formal insurance mechanisms, and family arrangements (marriages). Once a risky event happens, people react to the incident and use the *coping strategy,* which includes dis-saving/borrowing, migration, and reduction of consumption and the selling of labor including that of children.

Table 1: Main Sources of Risk

Type of Risk	Idiosyncratic		Covariant
	Micro ◄———— Meso		Macro ————►
Natural		Rainfall, Landslide Volcanic eruption	Earthquake, Flood Drought, High Winds
Health	Illness, Injury, Death, Disability, Old age	Epidemic	
Social	Crime, Domestic violence	Terrorism ,Gang activity	Civil strife, War, Social upheaval
Economic		Unemployment Resettlement Harvest failure	Changes in food prize Growth collapse Hyperinflation Financial crisis Technology shock Terms of trade Transition costs of economic reforms
Political		Riots	Political default on social programs, Coup d'etat
Environment		Pollution, Deforestation, Nuclear disaster	

Source: World Bank, 2001.

All these risks can have a direct impact on the social well being of individuals. An effective management of sharing these risks, therefore, could alleviate the consequences of poverty, or even propel people to seek ways out of the poverty trap, i.e. through saving and credit options. A professional Social Risk Management (SRM) is, for several reasons, an important issue for sustainable rural development as Holzmann and Jørgensen (2000) point out:

- Welfare enhancing: SRM reduces the vulnerability of the poor, improves the consumption smoothing and increases the equity;

- Economic development and growth aspects: SRM and a smoothed consumption will lead households to engage in high-risk and high-yield activities, improve the effectiveness and costs for informal provisions;

- Poverty reduction: SRM reduces and prevents transitory poverty. It likewise provides instruments to overcome poverty.

Effective SRM includes several actors taking different responsibilities down from the macro- to the micro levels. While in developed economies people can strongly rely on public action in case of facing serious calamities, the poor in less developed countries often have to trust solely on traditional and self-organized systems of social protection.

2.2. Players in Rural Risk Sharing

Basically, four main actors can be found, more or less present in rural areas depending on the level of development (Jütting, 2000):

- the public sector

- the private-for profit sector

- community-based organizations

- the household

The two latter actors are regarded as the backbone of rural risk management instruments. Community-based organizations are civic associations. They are non-profit oriented and have their roots in the local community. They provide social services, provide insurance, credit, or saving products and offer the target group the opportunity to formulate their needs and interests. Cooperation within these civic organizations functions as *"episodic or long-term and intergenerational, framed by norms of exchange and reciprocity, mediated by rules and institutions which may not assume concrete organization forms"*. (Robinson and White, 1997, p.6) All four actors use different incentives to ensure cooperation and compliance in the context of the principal agent problem. (Van Til, 1987) The public sector, as the central government or local government, forces cooperation with the rule of law and regulations and coercion. However, whenever able and necessary, it also provides non-bureaucratic welfare to those who are in need. On the other hand, the private sector, as insurance companies or private-for-profit firms, depends on individual contracts with customers, which are judicially enforceable. Community-based organizations also rely mainly on self-interests of the people, their local affiliation, solidarity, social norm and values. The household reckons with strong family ties, their social norms and values within the family. (Jütting, 2002) The strength of risk sharing arrangements on household or community-based organization level lies in the better knowledge about private information of their risk sharing partners. Social norms, social pressure and social control are the main advantages. Government and private-for-profit insurance providers, on the other hand, have a lack of private information, which makes it difficult to estimate the actual risk and the possible financial consequences when offering risk protection products to disadvantaged groups in rural areas. To avoid moral hazard and adverse selection access to private information, it is essential to employ successful product tailoring. Lack of private information leads to the absence of the public and private for-profit-sector in rural risk sharing, which results in market and policy failure due to high transaction costs. (Jütting, 2002)

2.3. Individual Strategies on Household Level to Cope with Risk

There is broad variety of strategies of risk protection in rural areas employed by low-income households. Risk coping can be differentiated in two stages: First, households often resolve their income problems by making conservative production choices and diversifying their income-generating activities. This is regarded as protection mechanisms from income shocks before they occur. Second, after suffering from a shock the household can ease consumption problems by borrowing money, employing insurance arrangements, or shift labor from farm to off-farm employment. (Morduch, 1995)

This section explores the role of the household as a risk-coping institution and illustrates the most important strategies of risk sharing on the household level. (see Dercon, 2002, 2003) Not all strategies summarized below are applied in each household. Depending on their living conditions, the social status and local environment mixtures of different approaches are chosen. The main risk-coping strategies on household level are:

- Marriage and Migration
- Self-help networks based on ethnic ties, kinship, sex etc.
- Diversification of income sources and accumulation of assets
- Taking informal credit and gift exchange

2.3.1. Marriage and Migration

The parents usually choose marriage of daughters to husbands and vice-versa in order to secure long-term interest. This practice is a long tradition practiced in rural areas as a safety measurement. These contractual arrangements are aimed at mitigating income risks and enhance consumption smoothing. An even more risk-coping strategy, especially for farm households, is the marriage linked with migration of women and men to another region to reduce the covariant risk. This constellation reduces significantly the variability of the household food consumption. Moreover, the economic contributions are also seen to be valuable in the context of the family and the village economy. (Becker, 1973, 1974, Rosenzweig and Stark, 1998, Bhattacharya, 2000)

2.3.2. Networks Based on Ethnic Ties, Kinship, and Sex

The reliance on networks based on ethnic ties, kinship, sex etc. are regarded as another important risk-coping strategy. Insurance based on reciprocity among households on the village level is not always an appropriate tool where an informal group could provide protection. This might apply to relatively homogenous societies within a geographic proximity. However, societies are often more complex and diverse and groups are often based on ethnic groups or castes. The fact that families at large have developed risk-sharing mechanisms is not new (see Kotlikoff and Spivak, 1981, Rosenzweig, 1988), but in some regional areas, kinship in general, and ethnic ties play a substantial role in the households risk management as Grimard (1997) illustrates with empirical evidence from Cote d'Ivoire. De Weerdt (2002) points out that the formation of self-help networks can also be based on geographical proximity, religious affiliations, and wealth. However, he concludes that poor households have less dense networks than rich households, which makes them more vulnerable in facing idiosyncratic risks.

2.3.3. Diversification of Income Sources

The diversification of income sources is a strategy to spread the risk of different income generating activities. In an eight-country study in West Africa, Reardon et.al. (1994) state that 39 percent of all farm households achieve a substantial part of their income from non-farm activities. Even agricultural activities are diversified. They grow different crops, or fragment their land into many parcels of land. They switch to profitable non-agricultural activities, which may be a difficult task and is limited by needed working capital or skills required. Therefore, the poor tend to enter into activities with low entry costs: firewood collection, charcoal production and agricultural wage employment. Richer households perform high return non-crop activities such as cattle rearing or small business involvement, which needs access to capital. Those with education can enter the non-agricultural wage employment market. (Dercon and Krishnan, 1996) According to these results, Collier and Gunning in 1999 argued that the poor perform low return-capital extensive activities due to the lack of capital to enter high return activities. Income generation, through high return activities, implies usually entering high-risk activities. The risk suffering from a loss is too high for poor households with the effect that they do not enter high return and high risk income generating activities. However, richer households can buffer these risks (Eswaran and Kotwal, 1989, Dercon, 1996) should a household suffer from idiosyncratic agricultural shocks by shifting labor from farm to off-farm employment to stabilize the income. (Kochnar, 1999)

Diversification of income includes child labor as well as long-term income diversification strategy or short-term strategy by withdrawing their children temporarily from school. This approach results in low human capital accumulation, which tightens the poverty trap for the younger generations even more. (Jacoby and Skoufias, 1997, Moser, 1998) Additionally, households hold buffer stocks, which can be cashed in after a risk occurred. Physical assets might be livestock, food or monetary assets as precautionary savings. However, these strategies face risks of inflation, theft, or diseases and reduce the households risk-coping ability. (Deaton, 1992)

It can be concluded that the poor stay poor, since they are constrained to low-risk low-yield agricultural activities. Therefore, to escape this poverty trap risk pooling or risk-mitigation, institutions should be strengthened.

2.3.4. Informal Credit Arrangements and Gift Exchange

Rotating Saving and Credit Associations (RoSCAs) are traditional membership-based organizations and can be found even in highly developed regions (Levinson and Besley, 1996) in very different designs and sizes. Those arrangements combine, as the name states, elements of saving and credit giving. Calomiris and Rajaraman (1998) conclude that some RoSCAs serves as an insurance device to cope with shocks and are an important SRM strategy option to smooth consumption. The basic idea is that the members regularly pay a certain amount into a joint pool, which is distributed either as a whole or in parts to the participants. In regular intervals, a different member of the group is selected by lot or bidding, until everyone has received the pool once. The position of the individual members changes, because depending on whether they have already received their share or not, they are considered credit takers or savers. This is why these associations are called "*Rotating*" (Bouman, 1977). Meanwhile, Adams and Canavesi de Sahonero (1989) remark that perhaps the "game effect" of the RoSCAs presents a value for the members in itself, because the point of time that the credit is actually paid depends on pure chance.

Results from the Philippines show that only 22 percent of households use formal credit. (Fafchamps and Lund, 2001) If the poor have the choice, they prefer informal credit and arrangements and gift exchange as compared with the formal one. Friends, relatives in the same or adjacent villages grant the vast majority of loans. Most lenders and borrowers granted loans before, and many have switched the role of lender and credit takers. (Fafchamps, 1999) The biggest advantage of informal loans is that they do not carry any interest charge and risk sharing can be achieved through repeated informal transactions based on reciprocity. Consumption smoothing is one of the main motivations for informal credits and gifts, but these instruments appear unable to provide efficient risk sharing within a village and not all shocks are insured. The quasi-credit in the context of informal risk sharing can provide a cost-efficient mix of credit and insurance contracts, which are enforceable, however, with restrictions to size and kind of risk. (Kimball, 1988, Coate and Ravallion, 1993, Kocherlakota, 1996)

While informal credit arrangements are mainly limited to friends and relatives, community-based micro-finance systems, and sometimes, insurance opportunities offer credit and savings to a broader defined group of people. The following section provides on overview on Micro-Finance-Institution's (MFI) different products.

2.4. Micro-Finance Institutions and their Role in Rural Risk Sharing

Micro-finance is defined as the provision of public goods, namely financial services, to the poor on sustainable basis with a strong focus on poverty reduction (Balkenhol and Churchill, 2002). Low-income households tend to trust more on MFI that are linked to local associations in which they already participate, than formal banking systems. Additionally, national financing systems are very often not available and if ever present, the interest is not affordable or the credit is not granted. Further, these institutions are very often regarded as distant and impersonal. The strength of micro-finance systems lies in the individual design of benefits to the target group, while traditional bankers do not respond to the day-to-day financial needs of the poor and have limited understanding of low-income communities' needs. (Preker et al., 2001, Balkenhol and Churchill, 2002)

Micro-Finance had its beginning in the Mid-1970s with the aim of reducing poverty through loans for income-generating activities. It began with the provision of credits to rural households as a productive investment for income generation. The saving option was called the forgotten half of finance in the 1980s while insurance was termed as the forgotten third part of financing in the 1990s (Zeller et al. 1997, Zeller, 1999). Today, all three financial components can be found in the developing world covering almost all basic financial needs of low-income households.

Table 2: Different Functions and Strategies of Microfinance

Strategy	Function
Micro-credit	• Risk taking (take advantages, avoid over cautious behavior) • Current liquidity management (smooth out consumption, increase choice) • Short-term shock (drought, famine)
Micro-savings	• Predictable live-circle events (education, marriage dowry, childbirth, death) • Capital formation (purchase of equipment, down-payment of land, growth) • Future liquidity management (smooth consumption, increase choice)
Micro-insurance	• Long-term income support (life and disability insurance, pensions) • Short-term income support (sick pay)
Financial intermediation	• Payment and money-transfer services (facilitate trade and investment)

Source: based on Preker and Jakab, 2001

The usage of MFIs has strong gender implications. Analysis of MFIs verifies that women are more reliable microfinance clients than men, take more credit, do more savings and pay the credit as contracted. (Goetz and Gupta, 1996) However, the same authors emphasize that men control a significant proportion of women's loans. Women tend to borrow and bear the liability for repayment, while men decide where to invest or how to consume the money.

While formal banks require security for granted loans, which the poor often do not have, micro-credit institutions had to rely solely on social capital and group pressure. This implies limitation in size and geographic dissemination and jeopardizes the financial stability of people in case of natural disasters or illnesses, which often hit a whole region at once and influence their ability to pay the corresponding rates. Micro-insurance in addition, suffers from epidemic illnesses, which as well affect not only the people's ability to pay the premiums, but also increase the demand on health care. It is estimated (Morduch, 1998) that only 3-to 5 percent of all MFIs worldwide are working on financial sustainable basis without depending on supporting external funds. Within ten years, it is expected that 7 to 10 percent of all MFIs can operate on a financial sustainable basis, while the other 90 percent have to close or have to count on further financial support.

The idea of MFI, especially that of providing credit to poor households generated many hopes (see Hulme and Mosley, 1996). It was regarded, as an effective instrument to combat poverty but empirical data on the success is hardly available except for some anecdotal evidence. The evidence of an overall positive impact of the credit component in MFI has yet to be brought. Only a few MFI received a strict statistical evaluation, since the overall impact is difficult to assess and is deemed as biased due to other policy interventions on the macro and micro levels, natural conditions as weather as well.

The Grameen Bank in Bangladesh is the flagship of the micro-financing movement. The bank serves two million landless borrowers and has a repayment rate of 98 percent with modest profits. However, on the other side of the coin, the Grameen Bank received total subsidies of US$ 26-30 million in 1996 (Morduch, 1999a). A cross-sectional survey of almost 1800 households with clients of the Grameen Bank, other MFIs and non-clients showed that those households with access to these programs have a lower variation in labor supply and consumption across the seasons compared to the members of the control group. Therefore, the most important impact of MFIs might be the reductions of vulnerability but not poverty *per se* (Morduch, 1998, 2000). Similar results are reported from Africa (Kenya, Malawi and Ghana). Buckley (1997) states that less than 10 percent of all credit takers from formal and informal banking institutions, were able to demonstrate any technological change in production since they received the first loan. The use of credits may reflect liquidity problems but not unsatisfied demand for credit, while results from Bolivia (Navajas et. al. 2000) show that MFI do not reach the poorest of the poor, but those groups, who were near the poverty line –

the richest of the poor. The Gertler et al. (2003) report from Indonesia showed that families who live far away from MFIs reduce their consumption more than families living near these institutions. Therefore, MFIs primary merit might not be the catalyst for more enhanced technological change, but rather a guarantor for improved social protection.

MFIs reach a much larger number of clients through saving mobilization than credit provision (Fiebig, Hannig, Wisniwsky, 1999). The savings are volatile and depend on high seasonality particularly those in the rural areas. Additionally, small savings as well as small credit cause high transaction costs, which need to be subsidized by external funding, since reaching the poorest of the poor is more cost intensive than other market segments. (Conning, 1999) The saving and credit option, however, provided by MFIs or informal credit and saving clubs can be regarded as another tool in the context of SRM. (Zeller, 1999)

Figure 1: Potential for Insurance as a Coping Strategy

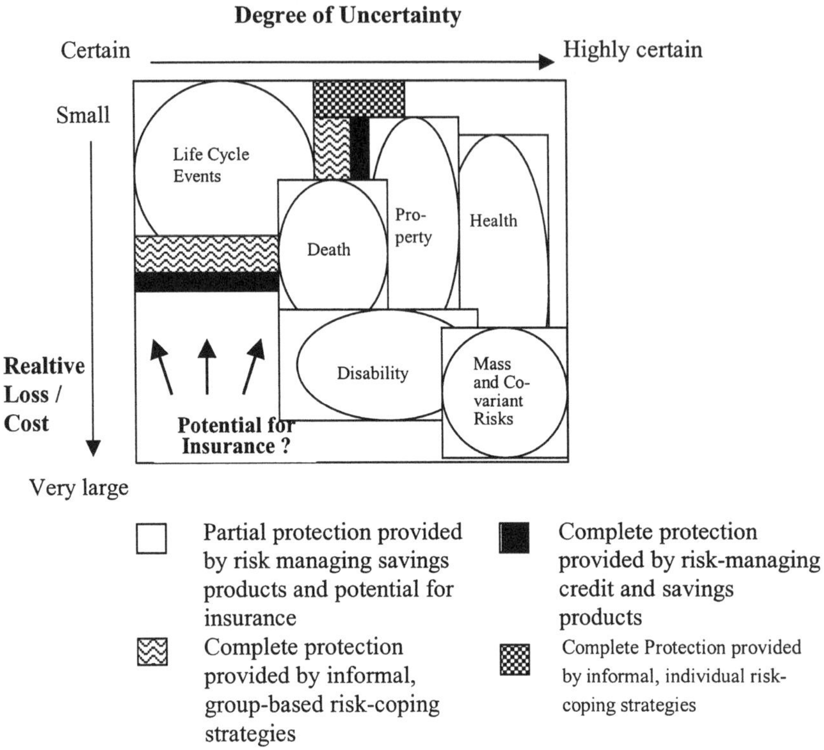

Degree of Uncertainty

Certain ──────────────────────────▶ Highly certain

Small

Life Cycle
Events

Pro-
perty

Health

Death

**Realtive
Loss /
Cost**

Disability

Mass
and Co-
variant
Risks

**Potential for
Insurance ?**

Very large

☐ Partial protection provided
by risk managing savings
products and potential for
insurance

■ Complete protection
provided by risk-managing
credit and savings
products

▧ Complete protection
provided by informal,
group-based risk-coping
strategies

▨ Complete Protection provided
by informal, individual risk-
coping strategies

Source: Brown and Churchill (1999).

As figure 1 illustrates, there is much room for insurance to fill the gaps in rural
risk management. Different risk management tools as mentioned above are
appropriate for different risks especially those that regard the size of the potential
loss and the degree of uncertainty. However, insurance is the most sophisticated
and complicated instrument in the provision of social protection.

Table 3: Typology of Insurance Examples in Less-Developed Countries

Type of Insurance	Potential for Insurance	Relative Risk / complexity to provide
Term Life	• Insurance repays outstanding loan balances upon death of the borrower. • Small face value policies designed to cover burial costs (can be either tied to or independent of loans).	Low
Endowment and Permanent Life	• Live-Savings insurance • "Dowry-Insurance" – policy for a 10-15 year term upon the birth of a female child. Provides fixed-term savings vehicle with insurance pay out if families primary income earner dies prior to the end of term. • "Retirement insurance" – similar to above, with longer terms.	
Property	• Insurance against damage, destruction and/or theft. • "Crop-Insurance" – insurance against specific causes of poor yields for specific crops. • Natural disaster insurance – with support from international re-insurers, coverage may be possible against some natural disasters.	
Health	• Accident Insurance – coverage against medical costs due to accidental injury • Curative Health Insurance – coverage to defray costs of medications and medical attention for specific illnesses and procedures.	
Disability	• Limited Disability – Insurance makes on-going loan repayments, if borrower becomes disabled.	High

Source: Brown and Churchill (1999).

Nonetheless, several insurance policies are available in rural areas, often provided by MFIs with long-standing experiences in offering financial services. Sometimes, even private insurers target the poorer groups with life insurance contracts as observed in the Philippine province of Guimaras during the field research for this study. In general, insurance underlies universal principles for its provision (Redja, 1998 as cited by Brown and Churchill, 1999):

- A large number of similar units exposed to the risk

  The pooling of risks is necessary to reduce the potential for adverse selection and calculating the average expected claims require a large number of risks to obtain statistically significant results.

- Limited policy holder control over the insured event

  This principle is not always realized. Moral hazard belongs to the most important problems insurers have to face.

- Existence of insurable interest

  Insurance can only be provided to those who have approved interest in protection. Otherwise, action could take place to foster the incidence of the insured event (moral hazard).

- Losses are determinable and measurable

  The occurrence of a loss must be verified and the costs must be measurable. Live insurer use death certificates, while health insurers rely on medical doctors. Determining the loss and the cause of an insured event is much more complicated for property insurers, since the proof of causality is less clear.

- Losses should not be catastrophic

  Covariant risks jeopardize the insurer's financial stability.

- Chances of loss are calculable

  Based on experiences of the past, the future likelihood of an insurance incident and its costs are more or less predictable. However, the calculated probability may vary from the actual occurrence of a risk. Calculations on probabilities are always retro-perspective.

- Premiums are economically affordable

  An insurance police is a "good buy," when the cost for premiums are less than the benefit offered by the insurance.

The spreading of insurance products for the poor is strongly related to the existence of MFIs, self-help groups or community-based organizations in a region, since the prevalence of insurance depends on large groups, which are all similarly exposed to a specific risk and on their ability to design and administrate such intricate product. (see Desmet et al., 1999) Organizations, which were able to collect experience in other areas of microfinance are more likely to succeed. Table 3 (Typology) visualizes different insurance options in rural areas with possible products with the increasing grade of complexity. The Self-Employed Women's Association (SEWA) in the Ahmedabad, a district in India, for instance, started with offering financial products as saving and credit option in the mid-1970s and extended their service to offering group plans for a Life and an Accident Death Insurance which was run and administrated by private life insurance companies. Another group plan is offered to cover the costs for hospitalization and maternity as well as Asset Protection Insurance and a Pension Scheme. (SEWA, http://www.sewa.org/insurance/products.htm)

The following section deals with health insurance in rural risk sharing in particular and the chances and limits of this relatively new tool in strengthening rural development. Most health insurance schemes cannot build up on decades of experience as credit and saving associations do, but the learning-by-doing process for rural health insurance has begun.

3. The Role of Community-based Health Insurance in Rural Risk Sharing

Microinsurance, rural health insurance, mutual health organizations are all under the umbrella of the term "community-based insurance." We use in this study the term Community-based Health Insurance Schemes (CBHI), since this term is widely used in the literature. CBHI, in developing countries, follow basically the same principles of insurance as those in wealthy countries (see previous section). This sections deals with problems and chances CBHI has to face – some CBHI can rely on more or less stable financial figures, while other struggle for survival. Many of the CBHI were founded in the 1990s, but some are based on indigenous arrangements such as the *eders* in Ethiopia for instance, which have a long tradition of rural risks sharing including those which are against the risk of illness (World Bank, 2002, Mariam, 2003). In this section, we will analyze CBHI's challenges and afterwards their role in risk pooling and contribution for the provision of health care in rural areas. First, we take a closer look to the different types of CBHI in the developing world.

3.1. Community Health Care Financing Mechanisms

A review of literature by Jakab and Krishnan (2001) identifies four different kinds of ownership of community financing to provide protection against the costs of illness.[1]

- **Community Costs-Sharing** is based on user fees to mobilize resources for health. This financing tool is based on out of pocket spending, although in this scheme, the community has set the level of user fees. Since pre-payment mechanism is not applied, community costs-sharing could be regarded as insurance by definition.

- **Community Prepayment or Mutual Health Organizations** are characterized by pre-payment, voluntary membership and risk sharing. The community involvement is strong regarding the design and management of the scheme.

- Another possibility to finance the costs of illness on community level is the set up of **Provider Based Health Insurance**. These organizations are run by single provider units as hospitals. They share the same characteristics as community prepayment organizations, but cover also catastrophic risks.

- The fourth and last classification of community health financing organizations are **Government or Social Insurance Supported Community Driven**

---

[1]   For different typologies see Atim (1998), Criel (1999), Hsiao (2001).

Schemes. These schemes are affiliated to formal social security arrangements or government-run programs. The community participates in implementation and management of the scheme that could rely on a significant financial contribution supporting the said scheme.

Different types of CBHI have been developed, but one common feature of community health care financing

"is the pre-dominant role of collective action in raising, pooling, allocating/purchasing, and/or supervising the management of health financing arrangements, even when there is interface with government programs and services in terms of subsidies, supplemental insurance coverage, or access to public provider networks." (Preker et al., 2001, p. 7)

The organizational structure and resource mobilization of community health care financing is one side of the coin. The other side is the allocations of the resources to health care providers. Basically, in low developed countries particularly in the rural areas, the same principles of payment mechanisms are applied like those in developed countries. The payment mechanisms share the same advantages and disadvantages regardless of the economic status of the countries.

Table 4: CBHI's Payment Mechanisms – Limits and Benefits

Payment Mechanism	Benefits	Limitations
Capitation Payments	Health-care (HC) provider motivated to minimize costs of provision. Insurer has certainty on claims expense.	• Difficult to convince HC provider to agree due to risk of over usage and cost escalation • Requires adequate control on quality of service
Fee-for-Service	Reduced complexity for the HC provider to determine prices	• HC provider encouraged to increase usage • Insurer has little ability to influence quality of care
Cash Indemnity	HC provider receives payment at the time service is performed rather than waiting until the end of the month. Insurer has ability to control which procedures are covered or not.	• Less accessible to poorer clients due to prepayment of large sums by the client • Higher transaction costs for both insurer and client • Limited motivation for HC provider to reduce costs
Fixed Cash Subsidy or Grant	Simple to administer for HC provider and insurer. HC provider receives payment at the time service is performed rather than waiting until the end of the month.	• Covers only a portion of costs of treatment, client is responsible for the remainder • Higher transaction costs for both insurer and client
Service Benefits	Virtually fixed costs for insurer; reduces complexity of estimating claims expenses. Insurer controls the quality of care. Insurer motivated to extend benefits to as large a population as possible.	• Requires capability to provide quality HC services • Requires greater volume of clients to reach break-even

Source: based on Atim (1998), Brown and Churchill, 2000.

3.2. The Chances and Limits of Community-based Health Insurance Schemes

A lot of research has been conducted on identifying the performance of various CBHI, but sound information on insurance for the poor is still widely lacking (Siegel et al. 2001). Most of the literature is rich in describing nature of the local variants of CBHI, but the evidence is growing that CBHI contribute in resource mobilization for health care and improve risk sharing of the burden of costs of illness. Due to its unique character and local adjustments, there have often been contradicting results among case studies. Likewise, there appears to be a complex task regarding the broad comparative analysis and development of indicators on benefits, financial resource mobilization and estimation on the overall potential of CBHI. Currently, there are different indicators, typologies and definitions that are used in the literature, which make it difficult to compare the strengths and weakness of the different CBHI. (Jakab and Krishnan, 2001)

There is no blueprint available to run a CBHI successfully and standard solutions do not meet the local necessities, since circumstances and objectives of a scheme can differ widely. Additionally, most CBHI have evolved in a context of political instability and extreme economic constraints as well as lack of good governance, which require individual approaches. Bennett and Gotsadze (2002) assume that many CBHI did not undergo an essential planning and evaluation process for an adequate scheme design during the start up phase. The lack of information on the target group and knowledge on the specific need for health care lead to design shortcomings. Consequently, mechanisms are not developed to avoid moral hazard and benefit packages are poorly defined. Moreover, lack of negotiations with providers on prices and an insufficient referral network leads to failures in premium calculation. As a result, one of the most important problems, which CBHI face, is financial management deficiency. A complex financial product as insurance needs comprehensive understanding in recording procedures of transactions and accountings and membership figures. These problems could also be observed during the author's research on Guimaras. (see chapter 7)

The problems CBHI have to tackle with are numerous. Many small schemes in rural areas, for instance, have to face problems like lack of supply of medical care. This is so because health care providers are situated too far away from the clients or they only provide rudimentary care. Those better off prefer those facilities in the nearest city and in private hospitals, which leads to decreased income for rural health providers. Consequently, this results in a "brain drain" effect and poor medical care. An overview of the drawbacks by Weber (2002a) summarized the most common problems among CBHI in Asia and Africa:

An overview of the drawbacks by Weber (2002a) summarized the most common problems among CBHI in Asia and Africa:

- Health care market failure
- Lack of supply and purchasing power
- Lack of information about prices
- Insurance market failure
- Lack of trust by the target group
- Lack of know-how, how to run a CBHI
- High transaction costs
- High drop-out rates
- Lack of sustainability
- Adverse selection
- Moral hazard
- By insurees and providers
- Corruption
- Failure of risk coverage

However, it is widely recognized that CBHI are able to mobilize additional resources for health care. Clients are more willing and more enthusiastic to pay for a CBHI than for general taxation, since benefits could be experienced directly. Further, it is assumed that clients would like to pay on regular basis affordable premiums rather than paying the fee for service out of the pocket (Conn and Walford, 1998). Poor households usually have the financial resources to join a CBHI. They likewise have sufficient savings that would enable them to join a CBHI as several studies including this (see chapter 8) have shown that the demand for health insurance, the ability and the willingness to pay is given (Asenso-Okyere et al. 1997, Asfaw 2002). However, the resource mobilization is not sufficient to reach cost recovery of the insurance (Pannarunothai, 2000). The ratio between salaries of professional staff managing the scheme and the relatively small amount of premiums make the achievement of cost recovery a difficult task. Cutler and Zeckhauser (1999) state that the main question in the discussion on cost recovery in health insurance should be focused on what could be achieved on health care and risk protection using a different spending strategy.

Another argument in favor of CBHI is the assumption that health care provision becomes more efficient and effective. Contracts with providers lead to a greater accountability in terms of monitoring the costs and quality of care. Further, contracts can specify what kind of health service is provided and the provider can concentrate to offer an efficient contracted health care. Therefore, the effect is that clients demand improved health care, because they can understand that quality of health care is related with their payments of their health insurance premiums, while competition among providers increases efficiency and effectiveness (Conn and Walford, 1998). However, high transaction costs connected with premium collection and administration costs in general jeopardize all approaches to increase efficiency. Moral hazard and supplier induced demand make health insurance costly. Moreover, competition among providers to improve efficiency and effectiveness is not given, due the low density of providers in rural areas. Also, efficiency in sophisticated management tool as monitoring, managing contracts, introduction of performance indicators resulting in increased efficiency are often not applied by CBHI. This regulatory capacity has to be developed through training and the adoption of business culture in CBHI's management style. (Musau, 1999)

3.3. Lessons Learned and Policy Implications

Setting up a strong government regulatory framework with national guidelines and a formal accreditation process could increase the proliferation and sustainability of CBHI. The implementation of umbrella organizations provides support during the design and implementation phase and also results in the familiarization of the staff with the administration of a CBHI. (Ron 1999, Bennett and Gilson, 2001)

Successful operated CBHI offer substantial benefits to the poor people in rural areas. However, the poorest of the poor can often not be reached even with subsidized premiums (Gilson et al. 2001) and the inclusion of this group can only be realized through social empowerment.

Key policy instruments to stabilize CBHI to improve the effectiveness and sustainability would be to increase the government subsidies on health expenditures to a substantial share for premium payment of low-income groups and the provision of health care (Bloom and Shenglan, 1999).

The governments should provide re-insurance against large expenditure fluctuations. Further, it is suggested that effective prevention and case management limit the expenditure fluctuations, while technical support should strengthen the management capacity of local schemes. Additionally, the links to formal financing systems and provider networks are encouraged (Preker et al. 2002).

The success of CBHI depends on various factors, which can be summarized as follows:

- Stable political conditions and supporting government action as financial support and clear policy framework;
- Analysis of the demand of insurance as well as the willingness and ability of the target group to pay;
- Community participation and "ownership" by clients;
- Promoting partnership with providers and government units on health care provision;
- Sufficient financial support from government or NGOs;

- Implementation of instruments to avoid adverse selection, moral hazard and supplier induced demand tailored to the local conditions;
- Sound management capacities including marketing by CBHI's staff;
- In-depth market analysis, product design and training of the management before setting up a CBHI.

Undoubtedly, CBHI are filling gaps in the context of SRM in rural areas. They play in important role in resource mobilization for health care while strengthening the protection against the risks of illnesses despite the exposure of uncertainties and challenges, which jeopardize its sustainability. Many schemes will continue depending on financial and technical support by government of NGOs, since the achievement of cost recovery would be a very ambitious target. However, innovative and individual approaches are required to strengthen this promising tool in rural risk management.

The following chapter deals with the most important theories on decision making under risk and uncertainty. Additionally, the impact of negative and positive incentives in the process of decision making will be discussed. Finally, the raffle model will be introduced to as a new approach in health insurance promotion.

4. Incentives and Social Health Insurance – a Theoretical Approach

This chapter gives an overview on different theories that help to understand the decision-making process under risk and uncertainty. Additionally, it will be shown under which condition individuals are willing to cooperate, and further, how the worldwide phenomenon of gambling, namely lotteries and raffles, and the provision of public goods can very well go together. Finally, a model of a combination of a health insurance and a raffle will be presented and the possible outcomes of this approach will be discussed.

4.1. Decision under Risk and Uncertainty - Gambling and Insurance

In daily life people often make decisions without any or less knowledge about its exact probabilities and outcomes. Very often, however, there is precise knowledge of potential probabilities available to individuals, which could be taken into account in their decision-making process. These include lotteries and many insurance contracts. Knight (1921) distinguished between *risk*, (which has precise probabilities) and *unmeasurable uncertainty*. Today, this determination is used by many economists as well as psychologists in dealing with decision theory. Keynes (1921) made a similar approach to distinguishing vague and clear probability. He distinguished between *probability* that represents the balance of evidence in favor of a particular proposition and the *weight of evidence*. This represents the quantity of evidence supporting that balance. In general, when an individual has to make a decision under risk or uncertainty, she/he has to take into consideration the known or estimated probability and afterwards weigh the value of the loss and gain and the desirability of the impact of prospective events.

People making decisions have to face both *risky* and *uncertain* situations, which refer to a reduction of possible loss as well as possible gain. Referring to the proposed combination of insurance and raffle individuals are uncertain, whether they become sick or not, but those individuals face a risky situation, if one knows the probability of winning. One might argue that the approach of offering a risk protection and simultaneously proposing to join a risky game of chance is contrary to the common perception that risk-averse (insurance) and risk-loving behavior (raffle) will not fit together. Those, who seek the security of insurance, will not tend to join a risky participation in a raffle. Vice-versa, those, who like to gamble, are not interested in buying insurance either. But risk-loving and risk-averse behavior is not a constant personal characteristic, and individuals do not get "boxed-in" in any of these categories. Friedman and Savage (1948) developed a model, which explains why the same individual behaves in a risk-averse way and buys insurance, but behaves simultaneously in a risk-loving way by placing bets on unfair gambles. They suggest that individuals will be risks-averse with respect to negative changes to their current wealth level. On the other hand, they are risk-seeking with respect to prospects that improve their social status significantly.

A review of literature on the behavior under the category of uncertainty shows what people have in mind when it comes to risky decisions. Quigging (1991) theorizes that smaller prizes offered in addition to the jackpot maximize the individual's utility and willingness to join. Golec and Tamarkin (1998) and Garret and Sobel (1999) came with their work and concluded that gamblers favor skewness of the prize distribution and not the risk *per se*. A large-scale field experiment in rural India was undertaken by Binswanger (1981) to measure the attitudes towards risks by poor people.

One of the most discussed experiments on ambiguity was conducted by Ellsberg in 1961. He found that people tend to be risk-averse, but the lower the probabilities of a given prospect, the more people are likely to accept unfair bets. An illustration proves this point: Imagine two urns each containing red and black balls. Urn 1 has an unknown proportion of black and red balls, while the second contains 50 red and 50 black balls. If you bet on the red or black ball, you get a payoff of $100, but if you bet on the wrong color, the payoff is $0. When faced with the gamble to put the bet on the red ball, most of the people prefer urn 2 rather than urn 1 with an unknown probability. However, this decision implies that the distribution of red balls is lower in urn 1. In a second game, the same urns with the same distribution were used. The individuals had to bet on the black ball and make their decision between the two urns. Again, subjects prefer urn 2, which implies that the distribution of black balls is lower in urn 1. Ellberg's paradox demonstrates ambiguity avoidance since people prefer to choose the unambiguous urn. But what exactly is the reason behind people's ambiguity aversion? Fox and Tversky (1995, p. 587) say it succinctly:

> "...that people's confidence is undermined when they contrast their limited knowledge about an event (urn 1, author's comment) with their superior knowledge about another event (urn 2, author's comment), or when they compare themselves with more knowledgeable individuals."

According to their research, they argue that this contrast between states of knowledge is the predominant source of ambiguity aversion.

On the other hand, another experiment by Ellsberg illustrates a preference for ambiguity (quoted in Becker and Brownson, 1964). 1,000 balls numbered from 1-1000 were put in urn 1, and in urn 2 is an unknown number of balls with any single number. Urn 1 has a probability on .0001 while all probabilities of winning are equally likely. The participant has to choose a number between 1 and developed a model, which explains why the same individual behaves in a risk-averse way and buys insurance, but behaves simultaneously in a risk-loving way by placing bets on unfair gambles. They suggest that individuals will be risks-averse with respect to negative changes to their current wealth level. On the other hand, they are risk-seeking with respect to prospects that improve their social status significantly.

A review of literature on the behavior under the category of uncertainty shows what people have in mind when it comes to risky decisions. Quigging (1991) theorizes that smaller prizes offered in addition to the jackpot maximize the individual's utility and willingness to join. Golec and Tamarkin (1998) and Garret and Sobel (1999) came with their work and concluded that gamblers favor skewness of the prize distribution and not the risk *per se*. A large-scale field experiment in rural India was undertaken by Binswanger (1981) to measure the attitudes towards risks by poor people.

One of the most discussed experiments on ambiguity was conducted by Ellsberg in 1961. He found that people tend to be risk-averse, but the lower the probabilities of a given prospect, the more people are likely to accept unfair bets. An illustration proves this point: Imagine two urns each containing red and black balls. Urn 1 has an unknown proportion of black and red balls, while the second contains 50 red and 50 black balls. If you bet on the red or black ball, you get a payoff of $100, but if you bet on the wrong color, the payoff is $0. When faced with the gamble to put the bet on the red ball, most of the people prefer urn 2 rather than urn 1 with an unknown probability. However, this decision implies that the distribution of red balls is lower in urn 1. In a second game, the same urns with the same distribution were used. The individuals had to bet on the black ball and make their decision between the two urns. Again, subjects prefer urn 2, which implies that the distribution of black balls is lower in urn 1. Ellberg's paradox demonstrates ambiguity avoidance since people prefer to choose the unambiguous urn. But what exactly is the reason behind people's ambiguity aversion? Fox and Tversky (1995, p. 587) say it succinctly:

> "...that people's confidence is undermined when they contrast their limited knowledge about an event (urn 1, author's comment) with their superior knowledge about another event (urn 2, author's comment), or when they compare themselves with more knowledgeable individuals."

According to their research, they argue that this contrast between states of knowledge is the predominant source of ambiguity aversion.

On the other hand, another experiment by Ellsberg illustrates a preference for ambiguity (quoted in Becker and Brownson, 1964). 1,000 balls numbered from 1-1000 were put in urn 1, and in urn 2 is an unknown number of balls with any single number. Urn 1 has a probability on .0001 while all probabilities of winning are equally likely. The participant has to choose a number between 1 and

1000 and decide from which urn she/he wants to draw the ball. Amazingly, most people chose urn 2 and it seems that in some situations, ambiguity is preferred rather than avoided. It seems that not only mathematically prospects influence the decision finding, but also the psychological processing of information of outcomes by decision makers.

Kahneman and Tversky (1979) observed different strategies that people follow, while evaluating the prospect of a decision. Often, these strategies were not based on mathematical logical considerations, but more on vague estimation and wishful thinking. One of the strategies the authors discovered is *coding*, which means that people estimate outcome of a decision as gains and losses to a reference point, which usually corresponds to the current assets. However, the description of the offered prospects can influence the consequent coding to the reference point and influence the expectations of the decision maker, as we will see later. Further, individuals *combine prospects*. They are sometimes simplified and their different problems and probabilities are combined. The gain of winning 200 with a chance of 0.25; and the additional draw of 200,0,25 will be reduced to 200, 0,50. In fact, the probabilities have not changed and the chances to win 200 are still 0,25. Additionally, the people tend to *segregate* the prospects with less risk from a risky component and simplify representations of binary choices. The prospect (300, 0.80; 200, 0.20) will be separated into a sure gain of 200 and a risky prospect (100, 0.80). This so-called isolation effect was observed later in other experiments (Cohen et al. 1985). People ignore mostly risky prospects in a multiple stage decision making process and put the focus on the less risky prospects. In general, individuals tend to generalize and try to detect dominance.

Individuals violate rational and mathematical decision-making and use the "rule of thumb" instead of calculating the chance. Research by Di Mauro and Maffioletti (2001) has shown that the possession of specific information about risks probabilities has only a weak impact on the decision making process on whether to get insurance or not. The valuation of insurance itself compared with those people who have only less or no information of the probabilities is almost the same.

As mentioned above, when someone has to make a decision (which implies the loss and gain of assets), the decision outcome depends on the individual's wealth. Kahneman and Tversky (1979) point out that the difference of a loss of 100 or 200 currency units (CU) appear greater than the loss between 1200 and 1100 currency units. The same phenomenon can be observed with gain of assets. But it can be shown that the attitudes to changes in loss of assets loom larger when being compared to its gains because most people have an aversion to a fair symmetric 50/50 bet. For low probability-of-loss events, individuals tend to be averse to ambiguity. But as the probability of loss increases, aversion to ambiguity decreases (Hogarth and Kunreuther, 1989). The aversion to a fair bet generally increases with the size of the stake as figure 2 illustrates.

Figure 2: Hypothetical Value Function

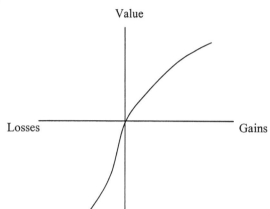

Source: Kahneman and Tversky (1979).

In summary, the value function is defined by its deviations from the reference point. Generally, the concave represents the gains while the convex stands for losses. The graph is steeper for losses than for gains.

Einhorn and Hogarth (1986) developed a model that is not based on a reference point (personal wealth), but on a so-called anchor, which means that, every initial estimate of the probability is based on past experience, data or an analogous situation. Then, the anchor is adjusted by imagining other values that could influence its probability. Faces the individual a high degree of ambiguity, the more alternative values of the probability are taken into account. It depends on the individual's attitude towards an ambiguous situation in particular, how weight is given to the alternative values of probability and whether they are greater or smaller than the anchor. This decision-making process can formally be described as

$$S(p) = p + k \tag{1}$$

where $S(p,k)$ is the assessment of the ambiguous probability, p is the anchor and k is the adjustment to the anchor. This model explains how people behave, when the prospects are not exactly known. This comes closer to real life decision-making compared to the prospects designed for experimental purpose. However, the Kahneman/Tversky and Einhorn/Hogarth approaches complete one another and do not exclude the other. Both approaches recognize that individuals make their decision not merely based on statistical reflections, but also on psychological information processing.

Kahneman and Tversky acknowledge that the desirability of prospects and a more psychological category influence strongly the decision-making. In short: Good impacts are desired, bad impacts are avoided. Additionally, it can be observed that very low probabilities are generally over weighted, as the following two decision problems illustrate:

(1) Assumed one has to make the decision between the *winning* of 5000 CU with a probability of 0.001 percent or a sure winning (100 percent) of 5 CU. 72 percent of the respondents prefer the first offer while the minority, 28 percent favor the second.

(2) Assumed one has to make the decision between the *loss* of 5000 CU with a probability of 0.001 percent or a sure loss (100 percent) of 5 CU. Seventeen (17) percent of the respondents prefer the first offer while the minority, 83 percent favor the latter choice.[2]

The first problem explains the mechanism of a raffle, while the second describes insurance. These two examples illustrate the propinquity of both phenomena, where only the signs were changed. Research by Cohen et al. (1985) has shown that individuals process information on probabilities differently depending whether choices are in the domain of gain or loss. On the gain side (raffle) probabilities are taken into account rather precisely, while in the domain of losses (insurance), individuals make their decision on the basis of vague categories such as "belief.'

The two decision problems mentioned above point to the non-linearity of the weighting function. The beginning and ending points of the graph in figure 3 show a discontinuity, which refer to the limited abilities of people to evaluate extreme probabilities.

Figure 3: Hypothetical weighting function

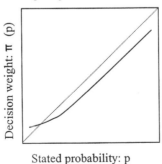

Stated probability: p

Source: Kahneman and Tversky (1979)

---

2   N = 72, example taken from Kahnemann, Tversky (1979)

Assuming that there is a preference to invest a smaller amount of money in low probabilities with desired outcome, this phenomenon strengthens the hypothesis of this thesis that a combination of a raffle and insurance work very well together. The distinction between pure risk loving and pure risk-averse person does not represent common behavior of people. Most people do both - buy insurance and join a game of chance. Due to the fact that the same amount of money has different values depending on whether the money has been lost or won, it is postulated that more people tend to join insurance than play a game of chance. The two examples above support this hypothesis. Further, it is hypothesized that the willingness to join insurance and a raffle depends on the current assets, since different wealth levels as shown above influence the valuation of the risky or uncertain event.

The decision theory gives insight in the individual's decision-making process, when the probability of loss and gain is known. Unfortunately, in daily life decision-making, this precise knowledge on probabilities is not always given, i.e. the probability of facing a serious illness. Decision-making can imply an interrelation between individuals with impacts on the behavior of the other person. The probability of a specific response to a decision cannot be measured. Likewise, categories such as "likely" or "unlikely" are often the most precise categories available. Making a decision in a two-person situation can be a bold venture, but uncertainty becomes even higher when an individual has to make a decision that influences a group of individuals, whose response to a decision has a direct impact on the decision-maker himself. We can find this problem for instance in group action. Decision-making of an individual in groups implies that one can only estimate the possible dynamics in a group and does not know whether the decision will be awarded, ignored or punished by the group. Groups in this context are regarded as individuals working together to achieve a specific target (Olson, 1969). Sometimes, these groups provide a public good, which benefit can be used by non-joiners or contributors. A public good is defined by the characteristic that once the public good is provided, individuals cannot be excluded from the benefit and the value of the good does not decrease if the number of users decreases as well (Nabli and Nugent, 1989). The following paragraph explains the dilemma of collective action and illustrates the abovementioned statement.

4.2. Considerations to Contribute to Public Goods

How people behave in social dilemmas depends on many structural variables such as size of the group, heterogeneity of participants, their dependence on the benefits received, the organizational level, monitoring techniques, and the knowledge transfer to participants (Ostrom, 1998). The outcome of health insurance in improving the people's overall health status, life expectancy, reduction of non-productive time due to illness and the experience of social security in alleviating the overall social development etc., has an overall positive impact on the national economy (Bloom et al. 2001). This can therefore be acknowledged as a quasi public good.

One of the characteristics of public goods is that most people want to benefit from it but are often trying to avoid any contribution for its provision. This could be called social dilemma or public-good dilemma. Those individuals, who want to benefit from the provision of the public good find it costly and would prefer others to pay for it. The result of this behavior can end in a non-provision of a public good. In a general sense, collective action refers to any problem that provides benefits and/or costs for more than the individual, so that coordination efforts are required (Weinberger, 2000). Collective action is the key element and the precondition for the provision of public goods, regardless of whether the collective action happens voluntarily or in a compulsory manner. A wide range of authors analyzed the problem of collective action such as Olson (1969) and P. Samuelson (1954). Other authors like Alchian and Demsetz (1972) worked on shirking responsibilities. Edney (1979), Grossmann and Hart (1980) put their focal point on the free-rider problem while Holstrom (1982) analyzed moral hazards and Geddes (1994) worked on the well- known prisoners dilemma. The complexity of participation in the provision of public goods has been analyzed by many disciplines, like experimental game theorist (Falk and Fischbacher 2000, Fehr and Gaechter, 2000 Güth and Yaari 1992), political scientists (Axelrod 1984), evolutionary theorists (Boyd and Richerson, 1988), sociologists (Cook and Levi 1992) and economists (Sonnemans et al. 1999).

Very often the benefit for a participant of group action cannot be measured in terms of monetary units. Some people feel a "warm glow", if they contribute more resources than others who benefit more from a short term basis (Adreoni, 1989). Other authors state that reciprocal strategy (tit-for-tat) is one of the key elements of collective action, but should not be mistaken with solidarity. Negative actions will be punished, while positive actions will receive a positive reaction. This simple and very basic norm is taught in all societies (Becker, 1990; Fehr and Schmidt, 1999). When individuals made the experience of reciprocity, people can acquire a reputation for keeping promises and will tend to perform actions with short-term costs but long-term benefits. In other words, a reputation of being a trustworthy person can be a value asset. According to Ostrom (1998), successful collective action is mainly based on trust, reciprocity and reputation, which result in a new level of cooperation, which benefit the group. These rules and values, which are learned early in life influence immensely the behavior in the decision-making process and affects whether someone is likely to participate in contributing towards a public good.

These basic characteristics of collective action are also the point of interest of experimental economists. Most economic models are based on the self-interest hypothesis that assume that all people make their decisions exclusively due to self-interest. However, some experimental economists believe that they have found the evidence for fairness and reciprocity in personal decision-making by analyzing the results of Ultimatum Games, Director Games, Gift Exchange Games, Trust Games and finally the Public Good Game (hereafter referred to as PGG), which scrutinize the "homo oeconomicus" (Fehr and Schmidt, 2001).

In a PGG-experiment, a group of people decides simultaneously how much of their endowment they are willing to contribute to a public good. Many experiments with repeated games have shown that the interest to invest into a public good decreases with the duration of the game. Once the cooperators have noticed that selfish subjects take advantage of their cooperation, cooperators decrease or stop their contribution payment. In a PGG, without the punishment option to tackle the free-rider-phenomenon, the dominant and most successful strategy is to contribute less than the other players or nothing at all to the overall public good. In other words: The most self-interest behavior in a PGG without a punishment option will make the highest profit. Consequently, the public good cannot be offered anymore[3] (Fehr and Schmidt, 2001).

The behavior in PGG, with the possibility of punishing selfish players, changes radically. After paying the contribution, every player will be informed about the payments of each group member. Those members, who pay a low contribution, will receive, for instance, punishment points, which will reduce their monetary payoff. This represents penalty payments just like what happens in real life situations. In the ordinary PGG described above, cooperation is close to zero, while the PGG with the punishment opportunity achieves stable cooperation rates (Fehr and Gächter, 2000).

As outlined above, punishment or the use of sanctions can be regarded as a *negative incentive*, which can change the personal behavior of individuals to con-

---

3   Mathematically the classical PGG-experiment can be described as followed: "*In the typical experiment there are n players who simultaneously decide how much of their endowment to contribute to a public good. Player i's monetary payoff is given by $x_i = y_i - g_i + mSg_j$ where y_i is player i's endowment, g_i her contribution, m the monetary payoff per unit of the public good and Sg_j the amount of the public good provided by all players. The unit payoff m obeys $m < 1 < nm$. This ensures that it is a dominant strategy to contribute nothing to the public good although the total surplus would be maximized if all players contributed their whole endowment.*" (Fehr and Schmidt, 2001, p. 7.)

tribute to a public good. In the informal sector in low developed countries *negative incentives* are not applicable by the state (for instance mandatory social security systems) due to high transaction costs. An innovative approach would be to introduce *positive incentives* to stimulate the decision-maker to join a group, to participate in collective action and to support the provision of public good. The positive incentive has the function that participation will become more attractive by economical means rather than non-participation or even free riding. The usage of positive incentives to their members is popular among large social groups to ensure collective action. Unions offer several additional non-collective benefits, such as insurance, welfare benefits or recreational programs to attract new members and sustain membership. Many car driver associations, for instance, offer their members breakdown insurance. It is assumed that a positive incentive, namely awarding, can have the same function as a negative incentive to raise the individual's cost-benefit ratio. There are many examples where positive incentives stimulate collective action, but can positive incentives boost the provision of public goods? To the best knowledge of the author this question has not yet been analyzed in PPG-Games or in any other game theoretical approach.[4] However, in real life, the use of positive incentives for the provision of public goods has been already practiced successfully. In Taiwan, for instance, the government introduced in 1951 an invoice lottery based on the receipts given by merchants and service enterprises to customers in order to increase the government's sales tax revenues. Each receipt has a unique number and is entitled to join the draw. Customers had began to ask for the receipt with the effect that shop owners were forced to buy cash registers which resulted in increased tax gains. On the other hand, the introduction of a lottery decreased the auditing costs of tax collection, since customers have insisted to receive the invoice to join the lottery (Ministry of Finance, Taiwan, 2003).

---

4   E-mail correspondence with Prof. Dr. Ernst Fehr, Institute for Empirical Research in Economics, University of Zurich.

4.3. Linking the Provision of Public Goods with Lotteries

We have seen that collective action will take place and public goods can be provided, if a coercive power reduces selfish behavior. It is hypothesized that positive incentives such as raffles or lotteries can have the same effect in stabilizing the cooperation rates. Olson's (1969) seminal work analyzed why individuals sometimes act together or fail to do so in social groups. He noticed that even if a group action would be the most rational matter for self-interest individuals, they would not act voluntary together to achieve the objective. Collective action can only be achieved in small groups based on trust and reciprocity, or unless there is coercion (social pressure or punishment). There are also times when some separate incentive is offered to the individuals of the group or on conditions that they will help to bear the costs of the burdens. All these come up in the achievement of the group objectives.

In very large social groups[5] individuals are willing to act together due to punishment or positive incentives. Where no compulsion for action is given a "selective incentive"[6] can achieve collective action:

> *"In such circumstances group action can be obtained only through an incentive that operates, not indiscriminately, like the collective good, upon the group as a whole, but rather selectively toward the individual in a group. The incentive must be 'selective' so that those who do not join the organization working for the group's interest, or in other ways contribute to the attainment of the group's interest, can be treated differently from those who do"* (Olson, 1969, p. 51).

Group action for providing a public good can be achieved either by punishing non-participants or awarding them. The awarding option, namely the linkage of lotteries and raffles with the provision of public goods, has been practiced almost worldwide ranging from small charity groups, civic groups to professionals and nationwide lotteries with billions US Dollars of cash flow. Lotteries are viewed as instruments to overcome the free-rider problem, which result in an under provision of the public good. Compared to other voluntary contribution mechanisms, lotteries increase the provision of the public good, and improve the welfare of people. Furthermore, it is assumed that the linkage of lotteries through the provision of public goods could increase ticket sales. This could be explained through the "warm glow" of helping the society. Player obtain a sort of psychic reward by

---

5   Olson defines very large groups as "latent" groups. These groups are distinguished *"by the fact that, if one member does or does not help to provide the collective good, no other one member will be significantly affected and therefore no one has any reason to react"* (Olson 1967, p. 50).

6   Olson defines selective incentives as those that apply selectively to the individuals, depending on whether or not they contribute to the provision of the public good (Olson, 1982).

the selfless act of giving even if no prize has been won (Morgan, 2000). In other words, the linkage of lotteries and the provision of public goods can be the moral relief to the excitement of gambling.

Experimental research (Morgan and Sefton, 2000) has shown that the public goods provision is higher when financed by lotteries than when they are financed by voluntary contributions. Of course, the ticket sales vary strongly with the value of the prize, and it can be observed that the ticket sales drop when the public good has no value to the subjects. This means that the public good that will be funded using lottery income has to be acknowledged by the public and will be regarded as useful and needed.

Alongside all the welfare attributes of the lottery mechanism combined with the provision of public goods as mentioned above, the disadvantages are obvious. It is assumed that the provision of public goods with the financing tool "lottery" crowds out voluntary cooperation. While direct donations to a public good would be most cost-efficient, the more cost-extensive lottery will be preferred. In addition, it is well known that the prizes and the administration cost of a lottery reduce the net spending for a public good. While lotteries raise the funding of public goods, it never happens for socially undesired public goods. Those that are deemed "undesirable" remain unfunded by lotteries (Morgan 2000, Fehr and Gächter 2002). Nevertheless, lotteries and raffles are an effective instrument to provide public goods. The main strategy of raffles is to collect financial resources and distribute the gain for the provision of a public good. This concept entitles everyone to wish to participate in the raffle to collect as much as financial resources. The following approach is not mainly based on an increase of resources, but also on an improvement of the coverage rate and to lower the drop out rates of CBHI. For this reason, the following model suggests that only those who have CBHI membership are entitled to join the raffle. The more people who join health insurance programs, the better the health status of the general population becomes. This results in more benefits to the overall development of a community.

4.4. Introducing Incentives in Social Health Insurance: The Raffle Model

Both the terms "lottery" and "raffle" are interchangeably used in the literature in order to describe different games. Basically, lottery is a game, where the participant can chose his/her own lucky numbers, while a raffle is based on coupons with a printed lucky number. The following incentive approach is based on a raffle mechanism. An incentive is defined as

"... an explicit or implicit reward for performing a particular act and is a broad-ranging concept, which can apply to groups and organizations as well as to single individuals, which may be internally generated from within the group, organization, or individual." (Saltman, 2002, p. 1679)

Incentives are widely used and common in the business world as marketing tools to boost sales and improve the customer loyalty. When talking about Social Health Insurance common marketing tools can sometimes be found, despite strict rules in the competition among private- and government-run health insurance schemes. For example, in Germany, the broadly accepted assumption is that the health market needs to be regulated. However, the regulated competition among health insurers or providers is desired by the authorities to ameliorate efficiency, cost-containment and consumer satisfaction. In Europe, this attempt of entrepreneurial behavior includes solidarity as well (Saltman 2002). Unfortunately, it can be observed that competition among participants in a health system is not always guided by the aim of improved efficiency and effectiveness of health care delivery, but of a rivalry of the allocation of available financial resources (Mörsch, 2002).

In low-income countries, where a mandatory health insurance membership is not feasible, and people can decide whether they want to join an insurance plan, incentives and marketing tools are feasible and necessary not only to attract healthy new members to avoid adverse selection[7], but also to reach the most disadvantaged groups. Solidarity with poorer or sick people is mostly not a major reason to join a social health insurance scheme. An additional incentive could improve the risk sharing and stabilize the membership figures. The introduction of the following raffle model is proposed.

The assumption is that the insurance number could have the function of a lot. Every paying member, upon passing the qualification requirement, has the opportunity to join the raffle. Qualifying, in general, means the acceptance of additional regulations. Dependants can help to fulfill the requirement, but only one award per household is granted. However, the participation in the raffle is voluntary for insurance members and an individual can choose whether they want

---

7   For the theoretical framework on adverse selection, see Belli (2001).

to participate or not. On the other hand, if somebody wants to join the raffle, he or she has to join the insurance. The following figure illustrates the procedure of participation:

Figure 4: Model of a CBHI Combined with a Raffle

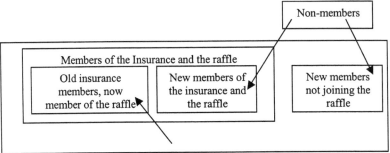

Source: Author's design.

The raffle participant can join the raffle at different levels depending on the regulation he or she is willing to join. In this study, a three-stage-model was developed. The minimum requirements to qualify for the raffle are defined in the first stage. These requirements should be relatively easy to fulfill in order to attract new members. In the second stage the regulations should be more demanding than the previous stage, while the conditions, which are hardest to fulfill, should be placed in the third stage. The value of the award rises simultaneously with the stage at which the insuree has qualified for. In brief: The higher the stage, the harder the regulation and the harder the regulation, the higher is the value of the possible awards. The following table is a visual representation of the three-stage model. Since the specifications vary depending on the local necessities, the terms of conditions have to be developed individually.

Table 5: Three-Stage-Model of Raffle Regulations Combined with a CBHI Scheme

Status	Terms of Conditions	Awards
First Stage	Easy to fulfill	Household or farming utilities.
Second Stage	Neither easy nor hard to fulfill	The value of the prices increases
Third Stage	Hard to fulfill	with the value of the lot.

Source: Author's design.

Formally, the raffle model combined with a CBHI can be described mathematically as follows: Let the known costs CBHI be T. The sum of individuals i voluntary contribution is (Σc_i). If $(\Sigma c_i) > T$ the CBHI can operate. However, CBHI is often provided, when $(\Sigma c_i) < T$ due to supporting payments by government or NGOs. In general, $v_i = b_i - c_i$ is the individual's valuation of the public good, where b_i is the individual received benefit, the personal experience of protection against the risks of illness and the improvement of the quality of life (see Wenzel and Laaser, 1990). According to a CBHI for non-members, the valuation of a membership is $v_i < c_i$, while for members $c_i < v_i$.

With the raffle, an additional positive incentive will be offered for both members and non-members. The individual's value of the insurance combined with a lottery is $v_i = (b_i + p_i) - q_i - c_i$, where p_i is the probability of winning the lottery, the value of the price, and the game effect. q_i is the benefit reduction and transaction costs[8] due to the raffle regulations. The valuation of an ordinary CBHI is, as shown above, $v_i = b_i - c_i$.

The economic success of this approach is given when the cost/income ratio between the income k_r, the cost of the insurance combined with the raffle, and T_r is smaller than the difference between k_{wr} and T_{wr}, which is the conventional costs for an insurance. Should the scenario occur that the costs increase with the effect of increasing membership figures, it has to be evaluated whether the additional costs can be justified. The following should be noted while conducting a cost-benefit analysis for the raffle model.

---

8   The attendance of preventive health education programs or the participation in vaccination programs may be felt first as an inconvenience. But the following improved health status will be recognized as a personal benefit.

"The ultimate goal of health insurance does not involve the usual economic concepts of prices, incentives and costs. Rather, the central objective of health insurance is to maintain and enhance our health. The payoff question, therefore, is what can we get for alternative levels of expenditure?" (Cutler and Zeckhauser (1999), p. 71)

In general, the costs of an insurance scheme can be defined as:

$$k_{wl} = (\Sigma c_i) + s - z - a$$

$$k_l = (\Sigma c_i) + s - z - (a + a_r)$$

where s is the external public or donated monetary support, z is the spending on health care, a is the administration costs, and a_r represents the spending on administration costs for the raffle.

It is hypothesized that the savings for the insurance will be higher than the necessary expenditures on raffle awards and additional administration costs. Based on this assumption, three outcomes are possible: First, higher membership figures could improve the ration of the full time staff equivalent (FTSE) to membership figures, thereby reducing the administration costs per member; Second, risk sharing could be improved significantly; and thirdly, medical care costs could decrease due to the participation of health education or vaccination programs.

In this study the demand of the proposed raffle model was analyzed and whether the target group would like to join or not. The following chapter describes the methodology that has been used.

5. Research Methodology

A demand analysis of the Guimaras Health Insurance (GHIP) was undertaken from January to March 2002. Guimaras is an island located in the Western Visayas portion of the Republic of the Philippines. The purpose of the study was to determine the determinants for joining respectively not joining the raffle within the GHIP. A structured questionnaire was designed containing sections on the demographic characteristics and personal notes of the respondents, e.g. sex, age, family status, income, education, health status, out of pocket spending, attitude towards gambling and their habits, opinions on the current health insurance scheme and the suggested raffle model. The structured questionnaire was adjusted to the local necessities and was reviewed by the Provincial Planning and Development Office of Guimaras. The Bureau of the National Statistical Coordination Board in Iloilo City reviewed the income section of the questionnaire and contributed valuable information about main income sources for the agricultural and the non-agricultural sectors in the Philippines. Moreover, the suggestions made by the SHINE-GTZ office in Manila helped in the design of questionnaire.

5.1. Sample Selection and Data Collection

For this survey, a two stage sampling technique was chosen. First, the villages (referred to in the Philippines as barangays) were selected. Guimaras has five municipalities and within each municipality, one barangay was randomly chosen for the data collection. The random mechanism ensured the variation of characteristics of the selected barangays - two are located near the sea which is far away from the provincial capital, San Miguel, with its main hospital (Cabano and East Valencia), while two barangays are located in the middle of the island near the Guimaras Provincial Hospital (Millan and Bugnay). The last barangay is located next to San Miguel (Salvacion) which is neither near the sea nor in the middle of the island.

Table 6: Population & Number of Households in the Selected Barangays

	East Valencia	Bugnay	Salvation	Cabano	Millan
Population	2308	1496	2411	3271	1328
No. of Households	459	305	461	592	274

Source: Provincial Planning and Development Office, 2002.

In the second step, a stratified random sampling procedure was used to ensure a 50/50 distribution of the members and non-members. The size of the sample was composed of 226 households[9] (115 member households and 111 not joining the GHIP). In total, data on the health status of 1142 household heads and their dependents were collected. The households were randomly selected from the household lists given by the barangay captain while the membership lists of the GHIP was provided by the organizers of the insurance. In each barangay, approximately 40 households were selected (20 member households and 20 non-member households). Many insurees, who were identified as non-members, stated during the meeting that they were in fact members of the GHIP. Those persons were then registered as members. The distribution of members and non-members per barangay, which was solely based on official statistics, was therefore inaccurate and not applicable. This procedure led to the fact that sometimes more non-members, respectively members, joined the focus group meeting. To ensure the 50/50 distribution, additional participants were randomly selected from the household lists and GHIP membership lists. Despite the use of a random sampling technique among the local population, the survey is neither nationally nor provincially representative.

In each of the five barangays, a focus group meeting was organized and a time consuming individual explanation of the raffle model and the GHIP (many respondents had no information concerning the GHIP before the meeting) was not necessary. The barangay captains contacted the randomly chosen households, and most of them attended the meeting. At the beginning of the focus group meetings, the participants had to register at the front desk. Those who were listed on the sample list, had to mark their thumb with a stamp-pad. This measure ensured that the research assistants could distinguish the sample members from visitors.

The meetings were set in the morning and took one to one-and-half hours. The participants were informed that the meeting had a purely academic purpose. All data would be treated as highly confidential to protect the privacy of the respondents. Furthermore, the participants were told that the organizers of the meeting would neither promote a membership in the GHIP or the raffle nor accept any contribution payments. Only information about the insurance scheme and the non-existing raffle model would be given and that afterwards, the participants were going to be asked about their opinions and attitudes regarding the said insurance and raffle option. After the presentation of the raffle model, the respondents were asked to wait until one of the five research assistants had interviewed them. The interviews were mainly held in the local dialect, which is called Ilonggo.

---

9   The term *household* is in equivalent used to insurance unit of the GHIP. In other words, the household is defined by all dependents, who are covered according to the GHIP regulations. By using this definition, it may happen that more insurance units (households) live under the same roof or share the same meal, which could not be observed in this survey.

Those sample group members, who did not attend the meeting, were visited in their homes the following day. The willingness to participate in the survey was very high and none of the household heads refused to be interviewed.

5.2. Development of the Regulations for Increasing the Value of the Lot

The regulations for the raffle model (table 7) were developed in a group meeting together with the officer-in-charge of the insurance, barangay health workers, and the insurees. After explaining the general purpose of the raffle model, the participants were highly motivated to develop the regulations and their knowledge of the insurance scheme. Likewise, local conditions and the institutional framework helped to adjust the regulations to the local surroundings. Finally, the group developed a raffle regulations design for the GHIP in order to meet the local particularities.

The insuree would have the opportunity to choose their raffle status between three levels (table 7). The levels were named "Bronze", "Silver", and "Gold" to reduce the grade of abstraction to the target group. On the "Bronze Level", the household members would have to recruit two new insurance members per year to gain the chance to win cooking and farming utilities. If the insuree wants to join the raffle on the "Silver Level", household members would have to participate in the health education or vaccination programs, which are suitable for them. For the "Gold Level" the member would have to pay an increased membership fee of 200 pesos instead of 85 pesos per year with the effect of increased medical benefits of up to 3500 pesos in case of illness. In this level, the insuree has the chance to win electronic devices such as radio, electric fan or cellular phone. Only one award is granted per family, even if more than one family member was qualified for the raffle.

Table 7: Raffle Regulations for the GHIP

Raffle Membership Status	Terms of Conditions	Awards
Bronze	Recruitment of two new members per year	Cooking and farming utilities
Silver	Participation in health education or vaccination programs	Livestock
Gold	Increased membership payment of 200 pesos with the effect of increased medical benefits of up to 3500 pesos	Electronic devices as radio, fan or cellular phone

The raffle model is individually designed for the necessities of Guimaras. Nevertheless, the basic idea of a raffle with modified regulations can be transferred to both public nationwide health insurance programs and local small-scale insurance schemes.

Before analyzing the demand and determinants why respondents would joined a CBHI combined with a raffle, we will take a closer look at the socioeconomic data of the Philippines in general and specifically that of the Province of Guimaras, where the field study took place.

6. Socio-Economic Overview on the Philippines and the Province Guimaras

This chapter will present an overview of the socio-economic situation in the Philippines as well as of the province of Guimaras that belongs to one of the poorest regions of the Philippines. This section provides us an insight into the specific situation and needs of the country and the Island of Guimaras, where the survey took place in order to become familiar with the local settings. Furthermore, we will introduce the Guimaras Health Insurance Project (GHIP) with its financial performance and benefit package to understand how the raffle was adjusted to the regional necessities.

6.1. The Philippines at a Glance

The following basic indicators for economic growth and health status are based on the latest data provided by the ADB, World Bank, UNDP, WHO, and the National Statistical Coordination Board of the Philippines.

The Philippines holds rank 77 with the Human Development Index[10] and belongs to medium human developed countries. However, the latest figures (2000) estimate that over 39% of the total population has incomes below the national poverty line. This represents an increase of 2.6 percentage points since 1997. Poverty incidence is lower in urban areas than in rural areas (19.9 percent and 46.9 percent, respectively). (UNDP, 2002) The high incidence of inequality and poverty leads to social problems with strong effects on the political stability and economic development of the country. Among the Philippine population, the gap between the rich and the poor income groups are still outstanding with a Gini Index of 46.2 as table 8 illustrates.

In 2001, the unemployment rate was stable at around eleven percent, which still belongs to the highest in the whole of Southeast Asia. The stagnation was partly the result of a slow creation of new jobs combined with a large increase in new labor force entrants associated with the continued high population growth rate. Due to the high unemployment rate and population growth, combined with relatively low economic growth, it is predicted that the incidence of poverty in the country remains unchanged in the future (ADB, 2001).

---

10   The Human Development Index comprises and weighs life expectancy. Illiteracy rate, as well the purchasing power of a country, has a scale of zero to one, one being the highest and zero being the smallest possible value.

Table 8: Inequality on Consumption Based on 1997 Data

Share of Consumption				Inequality Measures		
Poorest 10%	Poorest 20%	Richest 20%	Richest 10%	Richest 10% to Poorest 10%[11]	Richest 20% to Poorest 20%[12]	Gini Index[12]
2.3	5.4	52.3	36.6	16.1	9.8	46,2

Source: UNDP, 2002.

The population has grown from 42 million in 1975 to 75.6 million in 2000. It is expected that the population will rise up to 95.9 million in 2015. In the future, it is predicted that family planning programs will succeed in reducing the increase of population. Currently the Philippines have a population growth rate of 2.4 percent, but it is presumed that this growth rate will decline to 1.6 percent in 2015. It is also predicted that the population under 15 years is shrinking from 37.5 percent in 2000 to 29.6 percent in 2015. Almost half of the population (41.1 %) of the total 75.6 million habitants live in rural areas. During the last decade, a strong population movement toward the cities could be observed. The urban population rose by four percent, while the rural citizenship remains on the same level. In average, 224 people have to share a square kilometer. Due to the high population growth rate of 2.4 percent all economic indicators based on per capita calculation would have a better performance with a lower growth rate. In comparison, the population growth rate for East Asia & the Pacific region is only 1.2 percent and only 1.1 percent for lower middle-income countries (World Bank, 2003; Asian Development Bank, 2001, 2002).

The Philippines achieved a Gross Domestic Product (GDP) growth of 3.4 percent in 2001 despite the global economic slowdown of 2001 and security problems in Mindanao in the south. The service and the agricultural sectors contributed heavily to the growth of the GDP due to their favorable performance. Agriculture remains important to the economy firstly due to its contribution to production and employment, and secondly, due to the fact that agricultural products are significant inputs to many manufacturing and service sector activities. GDP is expected to expand by 4 percent in 2002, with higher private consumption and improved exports. In 2003, the GDP growth could increase by 4.5 percent, since an expected global economic recovery could take place and the economy begins to reap the returns from ongoing economic and fiscal reform efforts (Asian Development Bank, 2001).

---

11   Data show the ratio of the income or consumption share of the richest group to that of the poorest. Because of rounding, results may differ from ratios calculated using the income or consumption shares in columns 1-4.

12   A value of 0 represents a perfect equality and a value of 100 represents a perfect inequality.

6.2. Health Status in the Philippines

The basic indicators in the area of health show that life expectancy in this country increased significantly from the seventies (1970-1975) from 58.1 to 68.6 years in the nineties (1995-2000). Newborns can expect to live 55 years (HALE)[13] in healthy conditions (males 51.1 females 59.8), while male and females at age 60 can enjoy an average of 8 and 11.9, healthy life years, respectively. However, there is still much room to improve regarding the access to essential drugs. Only 50 -79 percent of the population can receive a basic drug treatment if needed. One reason might be the relatively low density of physicians with only 123 medical doctors per 100,000 people. Also, most of the physicians are located in Metro Manila and other regional major cities while less physicians are located in the re-mote rural areas. Eighty-three (83) percent of all born children in the Philippines receive natal care, while in 53 percent of all deliveries a skilled birth attendant is present. Twenty-eight (28) percent of all deliveries occur in health facilities. The infant mortality rate is 30 deaths per 1,000 live births in 2000 and the under-five mortality is reported at 40 per 1,000 live births (World Health Organization 2003, United Nations Development Program, 2002).

The overall spending for health care is 37 US$ (PPP) per capita. Most of the expenses for health care in the Philippines are covered by private sources (2.1 percent of the GDP), while the public health care expenditure reaches only 1.6 percent. In the year 1999, 108,300 million pesos were spent for health care (National Statistic Health Coordination Board, 2001). Out of pocket spending for health care is the most common way of financing the costs of illness (table 9). Only 4.8 percent of the health care expenditure is covered by a social insurance, while the government pays 37.9 percent. These figures demonstrate the need to strengthen fair health care financing mechanisms to ensure affordable medical treatments for the broader population.

---

13   Healthy life expectancy (HALE) is based on life expectancy, but includes an adjustment for time spent in poor health. This indicator measures the equivalent number of years in full health that a newborn child can expect to live based on the current mortality rates and prevalence distribution of health states in the population.

Table 9: Total Health Care Expenditure per Sector in 1999

Government	**37.9**
National	20
Local	17.8
Social Insurance	**4.8**
PhilHealth	4.6
Employee's compensation	0.3
Private Sources	**57.2**
Private Insurance (out of pocket)	46.3
HMO's	2.1
Employer based plans	3.8
Private schools	4
Others	1
All sources	**100**

Source: National Statistic Health Coordination Board, 2001.

The main leading causes of mortality in the Philippines are heart disease and diabetes. These are strongly connected to a person's behavior or lifestyle as the following table shows.

Table 10: Ten Leading Causes of Mortality in the Philippines (1998)

Cause	Male	Female	Total Number	Rate	% of Total Deaths
1. Diseases of the heart	32,3	23,6	55,8	76.3	15.8
2. Diseases of the vascular system	23,7	17,7	41,4	56.6	11.7
3. Pneumonia	17,6	16	33,7	46.1	9.5
4. Malignant Neoplasm	17,5	14,6	32	43.9	9.1
5. Accidents	24,2	5,7	29,8	40.8	8.5
6. Tuberculosis, all forms	18,8	9,2	28,	38.3	7.9
7. Chronic obstructive pulmonary diseases and allied conditions	9,5	4,8	14,2	19.5	4.0
8. Diabetes Mellitus	4,3	4,6	8,8	12.1	2.5
9. Other diseases of the respiratory system	3,8	3,7	7,5	10.3	2.1
10. Nephritis, nephritic syndrome and nephrosis	4,4	3	7,5	10.2	2.1

Rate/100,000, Population & Percentage

Source: Department of Health, 2003.

We will see in the next chapter that the main leading causes of mortality differ greatly in the Province of Guimaras. The reason for this difference might be poorer living conditions in Guimaras and inadequate medical infrastructure compared with other of regions of the Philippines which have better living conditions. The next section provides information on the situation in the province regarding the health status of the population as well its overall economic condition.

6.3. The Province of Guimaras

The Province of Guimaras is a small island located in the Western Visayas portion of the Philippines. It has a size of 60 hectares, where 54 percent of the land is classified as agricultural area, while the remaining land is classified as grassland, forest, wetland, and residential areas. The topography of the island is sloping to rolling with land elevation of up to 300 m above sea level. The main cultivated products are rice, coconuts and mangoes. Small farmers prefer rice and coconuts while cooperatives or companies are into the more organized system of mango production. Those households, who live along the shoreline, earn their income by fishing. Despite the excellent preconditions of the island for tourism, Guimaras has yet to develop its own local tourism industry in order to attract high-paying foreign tourists. The province is divided into five municipalities and 96 barangays, the smallest administrative unit in the Philippines. In 1995 the province had a population of 141,000 people, who live in 27.465 households. Most of the people live rural areas (109, 900 or 86,6 percent), and urban areas (16,570 or 13,1 percent) with a density of 234 habitants per square kilometer (Provincial Planning and Development Office, 2001).

Table 11: Population of Guimaras by Municipalities

Municipality	1997	1998	1999	2000	2001	2002
Buenavista	39.017	39.749	40.480	41.215	41.944	42.675
Jordan	26.513	27.152	27.790	28.431	29.090	29.749
Nueva Valencia	27.763	28.112	28.460	28.810	29.141	29.473
San Lorenzo	19.048	19.335	19.621	19.909	20.187	20.466
Sibunag	18.620	19.074	19.526	19.983	20.451	20.920
Total	130.961	133.422	135.877	138.348	140.813	143.283

Source: Weber, (2002).

In 1992, Guimaras became a full-pledged province and had an increase in economic and developmental activities bringing with it opportunities for employment and increased income. Those, who left the island earlier, came back and people from neighboring provinces also began to settle. This led to a growth rate of 3.24 percent in 1993 compared to the average growth rate of 2.43 percent (1995-2000). Since 1970, the population of Guimaras has nearly doubled from 73,000 to

143,000 in 1995. The population of Guimaras is relatively young. Thirty-nine (39) percent of the population is younger than 15 years, while 47. 5 percent are is within the 15 – 49 age group and the remaining 13 percent are over 50 years. (Provincial Planning and Development Office, 2001)

Most of the household heads earn their income from agricultural activities (59 percent) or they are either employed in the service (31 percent) or in the industrial (10 percent) sectors. The Province of Guimaras belongs to the poorest regions in the Philippines, where 75 percent of the households fall below the poverty line and the malnutrition is high, standing at 40 percent. The island has an unemployment rate of 14.5 percent and a visibly unemployment rate of 27.8 percent. In 1997, the average family income was 62.292 pesos, where 52 percent was spent for food and 4.1 percent for health care (Provincial Planning and Development Office, Guimaras, last available data from 1995 – 2001 and National Statistic Coordination Board, without year).

6.4. Health Status in Guimaras

In 2000, 2.797 total live births in Guimaras were counted, which represents a Crude Birth Rate (CBR) of 20.63 / 1.000 population implying that about 5.3 percent were low birth weights. In 2000, the Crude Death Rate (CDR) was recorded at 3.6 / 1.000 population with 487 deaths. The Infant Mortality Rate (IMR) was 5.4 / 1,000 live births and the neonatal deaths 0.7 / 1,000 live births (Provincial Health Office, 2001). The leading causes of morbidity are those, which would be mostly easy to treat. Table 12 shows the improvements made in combating pneumonia, diarrhea, tuberculosis (TB) and typhoid, while patients suffering from hypertension are increasing.

The respondents participating in the survey, however, suffer from different illnesses than the reported cases above. Most people suffered from influenza (37.9 percent) followed by bronchitis (7.7 percent) and tuberculosis and heart diseases (both 5.3 percent). This statistic has to be interpreted with caution, since the category "other injuries" accounts for 32 percent of the answers due to general statements by the respondents like "fever" or "pain in the abdomen."

Table 12: Morbidity, Leading Causes (2000)

Causes	5 year average (1995-1999)		2000	
	No.	%	No.	%
1. Pneumonia	2.297	27,6	1,628	22.7
2. Diarrhea	1.988	23,9	1,441	20.1
3. Bronchitis/Bronchiolitis	1.010	12,1	1,015	14.1
4. Hypertension	628	7,5	878	12.2
5. TB Respiratory	886	10,6	635	8.8
6. Conjunctivitis	60	0,7	449	6.3
7. Typhoid & Paratyphoid	474	5,7	355	4.9
8. Diseases of the heart	633	7,6	330	4.6
9. Parasitism	103	1,2	304	4.2
10. Chickenpox	249	3,0	142	2.0
Total	8.328	100	7,177	100.0

Source: Provincial Health Office, 2001. Reported cases.

In 2000, the number of cardiovascular accidents causing mortality increased, while patients with infectious diseases such as pneumonia and TB remain stable.

Table 13: Mortality, Leading Causes (2000).

Causes	5 year average (1995–1999)		2000	
	No.	%	No.	%
1. Cardiovascular Accident	69	18,3	108	27.4
2. Pneumonia	72	19,1	71	18.0
3. Tuberculosis	41	10,9	53	13.5
4. Cancer	49	13,0	49	12.4
5. Coronary Artery Disease	33	8,8	34	8.6
6. Hypertensive Vasc. Disease	54	14,3	27	6.9
7. Septicemia	17	4,5	13	3.3
8. Accidents	21	5,6	9	2.3
9. Diabetes Mellitus	8	2,1	8	2.0
Peptic Ulcer	4	1,1	8	2.0
10. Stab Wound	2	0,5	7	1.8
Status Asthmaticus	7	1,9	7	1.8
Total	377	100	394	100

Source: Provincial Health Office, 2001. Reported cases.

The province has three hospitals, one in Jordan and in Buenavista and an extension in Nueva Valencia. Altogether, 65 hospital beds are available. The provincial hospital has been upgraded recently with a total loan of 3 million pesos, provided by the World Bank, while the hospital in Nueva Valencia is newly constructed (Weber, 2002). The hospitals offer basic medical care as well as x-ray, ultrasound, and ECG treatments. Nineteen government physicians and five government dentists are serving the patients. Each municipality offer the patients a Rural Health

Unit, while almost every barangay has its own barangay health center, 80 health centers in total, with 629 barangay health workers with limited medical skills (Provincial Planning and Development Office, 2001). For major diseases, the patients are referred to providers or hospitals in Iloilo, a city with 300,00 inhabitants on the neighboring island of Panay (currently about 20 percent of the cases). There are two government hospitals and several private clinics. Since not all drugs are available in Guimaras, patients with less common diseases have to obtain their medicines from Iloilo. This means long travel distances connected with additional transportation costs for patients and their relatives.

Besides the GHIP, several other health insurance options are available in Guimaras. To become a PhilHealth member under the indigent program would be the most expensive choice. This program has a contribution of 1188 pesos annually offering a broad benefit package. The other option is to become a member of one of the three other health insurance schemes, which are all connected with a cooperative. The schemes are open even to those, who are not members of the cooperative. The annual contribution lies between 60 and 120 pesos a year. All schemes concentrate their benefit package on hospitalization, "catastrophic" illnesses and drugs. None of the schemes do appear financially jeopardized, since they make a large surplus. However, there is no separate bookkeeping between the health insurance finance and the cooperative bookings. The GHIP is the market leader on Guimaras as the following table shows:

Table 14: Health Insurance Coverage on Guimaras

	PhilHealth	GHIP	Other schemes	Covered
Paying members	3.480	6.076	2.508	12.064
Dependants	7.788	18.228	7.524	33.540
Total	11.268	24.304	10.032	45.604

Source: Provincial Planning and Development Office, 2002.

With a population of 143,000 people, less than one-third is covered by health insurance. There is much room for improvements concerning the health insurance coverage rate among the population. It is estimated that the total health expenditure in the province is about 150 million pesos. Fifty-three (53) percent of the health expenditure is financed by the national, province or municipality sources, while 43 percent is paid out of the pocket by the patients. The expenditure is spent mostly in the form of drugs, private hospitals and payments for doctors in Iloilo. In 2000, the GHIP paid benefits to its members 331,512 pesos, which is less than one percent of the total health spending in Guimaras. (Weber 2002) The following chapter provides a deeper insight to the GHIP in so far as the performance of the scheme, past achievements and the future challenges are concerned.

7. The Guimaras Health Insurance Project

The planning of a Social Health Insurance for the poor in Guimaras began in the mid-seventies. In 1976, a program called Medicare II was started in the municipality of Nueva Valencia as a pilot project. To offer medical care to insurees, a hospital was built in this municipality. In 1992, the Philippine Medical Care Commission evaluated the project's viability and came to the conclusion that a province-wide implementation of the program would be possible. One year later, the GHIP was founded by the Philippine Medical Care Commission and the Province of Guimaras, after which a memorandum of the implementation of a social health insurance was signed (Integrated Community Health Service Project, 2002). This agreement had the purpose of responding to the need to expand coverage and to include those, who are not covered by programs targeting the formal and employed sector. Currently, the GHIP is organized and administrated by the Provincial Government with the Governor as the head in charge. This chapter provides an overview on the GHIP itself, the performance and coverage of the GHIP.

7.1. Financial Facts and Figures

Data concerning the GHIP was collected using a combination of expert interviews with the leading personnel. It also contains an analysis of the key documents obtained from the insurance, such as their reports or indicators of financial and management performance, information on the benefit package and, in general, the structure of the insurance. A list of the needed indicators was provided to the organizers. The officials delivered a Summary Report (1993-2000) containing data about the income, disbursements, claims, membership figures and the utilization rate. Profound figures on the membership were not available.

While studying the membership and financial statistics of the GHIP, many questions have arisen concerning the accuracy of the data. A report provided by the GHIP shows more than 70,000 beneficiaries. The figures in the same report reveals that that contract renewals and new members show only 2,000 members with approximately 6,000 paying members. This dilemma could not be solved during the data evaluation in Guimaras. One indicator used to get an idea of the membership's size is the annual collected contribution. Since the annual contribution fee per household is known, the number of paying members can be estimated. Due to the vague character of the obtained information, the other indicators based on the membership figures, i.e. utilization rate, can only be estimated with limited certainty.

Based on this assumption outlined above, it is estimated that the GHIP has 5770 paying members in 2000 with 18200 dependants, which covers 17 percent of the population of Guimaras.

Table 15: GHIP Membership Statistics based on GHIP Data

	1993	1994	1995	1996	1997	1998	1999	2000
Balance previous year	0	1.445	7.154	6.552	8.132	7.358	7.861	5.770
New	1.445	6.539	3.156	3.980	2.167	1.955	971	720
Dropped	0	-830	-3.758	-2.400	-2.941	-1.452	-3.062	-414
Balance	1.445	7.154	6.552	8.132	7.358	7.861	5.770	6.076
Dependants (estimated)	4.335	21.462	19.656	24.396	22.074	23.583	17.310	18.228
Total	5.780	28.616	26.208	32.528	29.432	31.444	23.080	24.304

Source: GHIP and own calculations.

The membership in the GHIP is voluntary and is not restricted to special target groups. Children of the household heads are included free of charge. In general, there are five categories of GHIP members:
• Regular paying members
• Indigents, who do not have to pay contribution
• Senior citizens, who are covered free of charge
• Barangay Health Worker (BHW), who are covered free of charge
• Dependants of all the groups mentioned above

The GHIP is open to the whole population living in Guimaras. After 15 days of waiting period and after subscription, the insuree is entitled to receive benefits. The insurees can chose between 3 plans -- plans A, B, and C, which differ in the height of the ceiling. Depending on the plan, the contribution varies. It ranges between 85 pesos for regular and 300 pesos for the maximum benefit. The municipalities and the province are subsidizing Plan A of the GHIP membership premiums.

Table 16: GHIP Contributions

	Members	Municipality	Province	Total
Plan A				150
Regular	85	25	40	150
Indigent	0	30	120	150
Seniors	0	75	75	150
BHW	0	110	40	150
Plan B	200	0	0	200
Plan C	300	0	0	300

Source: GHIP, in pesos.

In addition to the subsidies, the government pays the wages of the coordinator and clerks, supplies, materials and transportation. Moreover, the GHIP uses office space in the hospital for free. All together, the payments of the member's represent only 25 percent of the income of the scheme, while the other amount are public subsidies. The GHIP has a huge reserve of more than 2 million pesos, which is almost about seven times the annual expense for benefits. Usually, a scheme of this size would need a reserve of 300,000 pesos to ensure liquidity (Weber, 2002). The reason for this surplus is the low utilization rate and the limitation of the costs per case of illness due to low ceilings. The reserve is kept in a bank account in Guimaras and controlled by the provincial treasurer.

Currently, the GHIP has a full-time staff equivalent (FTSE) of 7.65. In other words, one full time staff serves 800 members. This is much for a scheme that does not have to handle complicated claims or payments. The total annual costs for salaries were 516,000 pesos in 2001, while the surplus of the GHIP was only 332,302 pesos. Would the GHIP have to pay the staff salaries out of their balance, the sustainability of the scheme would be jeopardized.

Table 17: GHIP Staff and Salaries

Staff	No. of individuals	Time used for GHIP	Full time staff	Annual costs per staff member	Total annual costs
Coordinator	1	30%	0.30	33040	33040
Municipal Clerk	5	50%	2.50	29700	148500
Encoders	2	100%	2.00	29700	59400
Billing clerk	1	100%	1.00	29700	29700
Nurse	4	20%	0.80	44480	177922
Administration clerk	1	100%	1.00	63132	63132
Doctor	1	5%	0.05	5000	5000
Total	15		7.65		516694

Source: Weber, 2002. Costs in pesos.

Despite the FTSE being so high, a sound solution to solve this problem would not be to reduce the staff. Even if the staff would be divided into half, the costs would remain too high. The disadvantageous proportion between the relatively high salaries for educated, professional staff and the very low membership payments by the poor causes mainly the problem. This problem is quite common among Community-based health insurance schemes (CBHI) and is one of the main reasons why CBHI are very often dependable by external aid. In the case of GHIP, the government is paying the running costs for salaries. Only a significant increase in membership figures would improve the FTSE / membership ratio sustainedly. The already hired staff could for instance, support information campaigns.

7.2. The GHIP Benefits

The annual contribution is 85 pesos ($US 2)[14], while the spouse and children below 21 years are covered for free. The room and board, professional fee, operating room, routine laboratory and ambulance are in general free in Guimaras. In case the patient is refereed to a hospital in Iloilo the GHIP pays for the medical expenses. In 2001, 99 claims were paid for referrals in Iloilo. This reduces the GHIP to an insurance, which covers only expenses for medical treatment for drugs, when the patient has to stay for at least 24 hours in the hospital. Additionally, the patient gets a discount on special procedures, x-ray, and ECG with a ceiling of 2500 pesos per treatment. These benefits are granted to every covered household member. Should another treatment for the same or different illness be necessary within the same year for the member or one of the dependants, the expenses for drugs are covered up to 20 days of confinement. Depending on the plan the insuree wants to join the GHIP, the ceiling for drug reimbursement varies as can be seen in the following table:

Table 18: GHIP Ceilings for Drug Reimbursement

Insurance Plan	Premium	Ceiling Ordinary Cases	Ceiling Intensive Cases	Ceiling Catastrophic Cases
Plan A (subsidized)	150	800	1.400	2.500
Plan B	200	1.000	1.900	3.500
Plan C	300	1.500	2.800	5.000

Source: GHIP, in pesos.

Catastrophic cases are defined as those that need chemotheraphy, radiology, dialysis, bypass, major surgery, and diseases such as rheumatic heart, massive hemmorhage, cirrhosis of the liver, encephalitis, miningitis, etc. Intensive cases are diseases that need intensive care such as tuberculosis, H-Fever, severe diarrhea, typhoid fever, cardiovascular, other diseases of the liver & kidney, caesarian, pneumonia, etc. Ordinary cases include diseases such as headache, skin diseases, vasectomy, laparoscopy, etc.

Experiences by people in the island have shown that almost nobody is willing to pay the membership fee of 200/300 pesos. The GHIP benefits can be summarized as follows:

---

14   Subsidized net membership contribution. For details see table 16.

Table 19: The GHIP Benefits

Medical Procedure and Benefit	Additional costs for the members	GHIP benefits
Room and Board	Free in Guimaras, but not in Iloilo	Not covered
Medicines	May be bought with discount	Reimbursement up to the ceiling, when longer than 24h in the hospital
Routine laboratory	Free	Not covered
Special procedure	100 pesos	10 percent discount
ECG	70 pesos	50 percent discount
X-ray	80 pesos	10 percent discount
Ultrasound	250 pesos	Not covered
Professional fee	Free in Guimaras, but not in Iloilo	Not covered
Operating room	Free in Guimaras, but not in Iloilo	Not covered
Ambulance	Free in Guimaras, but not in Iloilo	Not covered

Source: GHIP.

The common phenomenon of moral hazard in voluntary health insurance schemes are not visible, since the GHIP pays only for an illness which requires a hospital stay of at least 24 hours. The hospital staff undertakes the gatekeeper function. This causes the very low utilization rate of the GHIP between two and three percent during the last years only.

Table 20: Claims Statistics GHIP

	1993	1994	1995	1996	1997	1998	1999	2000
Beneficiaries	5780	28616	26208	32528	29432	31444	23080	24304
Claims filed	54	525	118	894	817	925	581	525
Claims paid	37	430	118	870	803	906	568	512
Disapproved	17	95	0	24	14	19	13	13
Utilization rate in %	0,64	1,50	0,45	2,67	2,73	2,88	2,46	2,11
Costs per case	308	400	3.827	554	551	579	661	647

Source: GHIP, costs per case in pesos.

The results of the analysis of the available GHIP documents show a health insurance scheme with high reserves and a very low utilization rate. As long as the government support lasts, the future of the scheme is not jeopardized. The most important problem the insurance faces is not the financial performance, but the low utilization rate and the stagnation of membership figures. Additionally, the height of the ceiling should be reviewed to ensure a significant reduction of out-of-pocket spending for health care. The raffle model can contribute to boost membership figures.

In the next chapter, we will present the results of the survey conducted in the Province of Guimaras. First, a descriptive analysis gives insight into the socio-economic structure as well as the health status of the sample. A willingness to pay and a willingness to join analysis complete the descriptive part. Second, the determinants for joining the raffle will be identified to estimate the likelihood of the different sub-groups (within the sample) in joining the raffle.

8. Results

In this chapter, the sample will be analyzed according to the socio-economic structure and the respondent's attitudes towards the raffle model. Moreover, the willingness to join and pay were likewise analyzed, with the latter being subjected to an ordinal regression analysis. Later, different binary probit models of partici-pation in the GHIP and the raffle will be represented to determine the household characteristics, which influence the likelihood of the respondents' participating in the study.

8.1. Analysis on the GHIP

Guimaras belongs to the poorest provinces in the Philippines. The average monthly household income of the households randomly selected for this survey is 3,354 pesos and 803 pesos per capita. The official reports states an annual family income of 62,300 pesos annually in 1997 (Provincial Planning and Development Office, 2001). The difference could arise due to different reporting or estimation techniques, i.e. definition of household vs. family, the official statistics, a possible under reported income by the respondents who were surveyed and/or the lack of universal representativeness.

Table 21: Household Income in Pesos

	N	Minimum	Maximum	Mean	Standard Error
Household's total income	225	180	15000	3353,6	2262,1
Household's income per capita	225	30	3963	803	667

Fifty percent of the respondents earn their main income through farming, while 21 percent are self-employed entrepreneurs, who belong to the poorest groups in Guimaras. Furthermore, eleven percent generates their main income as a service worker. The average household size of the sample has five members. The sanitary conditions vary from "wrap and throw" (4%), earth closet (48,2%) to sealed water toilets (46,7). All respondents answered that they use potable water for drinking and cooking every day. Most of the respondents were female (65.5%) since women in Guimaras usually spend their time at home taking care of the household and children while men are the breadwinners. Both, men and women, were de-fined as household heads.

8.1.1. Necessity for a Health Insurance on Guimaras

Collecting data on the health status always pose the problem of the definition of health and illness. Until now, there is no broadly accepted definition of health and illness. This depends on a lot of variables and viewpoints. The medical, sociological or religious-cultural aspects are some of the basis for a definition (v. Troschke, 1998). In this survey, the respondents were asked about their individual health status and whether they have suffered any serious illness. The answers are naturally subjective and come closer to a sociological rather than a medical definition of health. Many respondents did not know the name of the illness and answered general descriptions like "something that has to do with the abdomen" or too specific descriptions as "I had tuberculosis for one day." This made it more difficult to find out what specific kind of illness the people suffer most from. In this survey, the variable "at least one household member suffered serious illness during the last twelve months" was taken as a reference point in analyzing the health status of the respondent's household. With this question, minor illnesses were excluded which are not covered by the GHIP. The definition of health, in this context, becomes not only sociological in approach, but also influenced by the benefit package of the GHIP.

Only 15 percent of the respondents answered that they are suffering from a serious illness during the last twelve months. However, almost every household (97.3 percent) spends money for medical treatment out of their own pocket and 41 percent spend more than 500 pesos during the last twelve months (figure 5).

Figure 5: Sum Paid for Medical Care (Out-of-Pocket) During the Last 12 Months

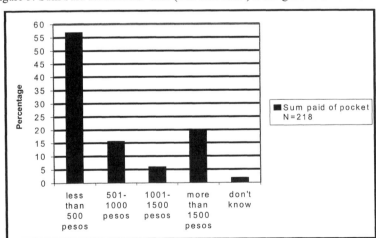

This means that the out-of-pocket spending constitutes a high financial burden, which could only be financed by borrowing money, receiving money from relatives or friends or by selling livestock.

Almost 50 percent of the households could cope with the out-of-pocket payment without any external help or selling of property. The rest, more than 50 percent of the households had to seek for credits and donations or even had to sell assets such as livestock to finance the costs of illness as the following figure shows:

Table 22: Financing the Out-of-Pocket Payment

No problem	Borrow money	Received money	Don't know	Sold Livestock	Total
48.2	35.3	8.7	0.5	7.3	100

N=218, in percent.

Figure 5 shows that the majority of the respondents had paid less than 500 pesos for medical care during the last twelve months. Most people can afford this amount without being financially jeopardized. However, only 32 percent would be able to cope with the cost of illness if the illness occurs in the next month (Figure 6). This means that in Guimaras the necessity for health insurance is given.

Figure 6: Affordability of Health Care Expenses in the Next Month

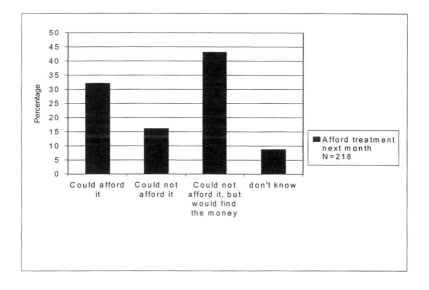

Those, who could not afford the same treatment in the next month (59 percent) were asked how long they would have to wait until they could afford the treatment again. Figure 7 explains that financial savings are not sufficient to cover health care expenses on a regular basis.

Figure 7: Time Needed to Afford the Treatment Again

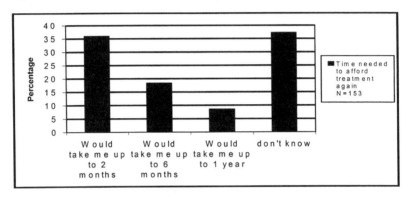

It has been set forth that the respondents would be theoretical in need of social health to cover their expenses for health care and drugs. Only minor treatments can be paid on an out-of-pocket basis, while more cost intensive treatments were financed by credit, sponsors or through the sale of property. Since the ration of the population covered by the GHIP could be improved, the question arises: Why does the target group not broadly accept health insurance?

8.1.2. Necessity for an Improved Communication Strategy

One of the main concerns, which CBHIS have to cope with, is the low coverage and high fluctuation of the membership due to relatively high drop out rates. For an effective risks sharing and protection, a longer duration of membership is desirable. As mentioned above the coverage of the GHIP is still low with only 17 percent of the population availing the scheme. One of the major reasons for this is that most of the non-members do not know about the existence of the GHIP. The communication strategy of the scheme has not yet reached its full effectiveness. Potential members can only make the decision to join or not to join the GHIP, when they have solid information on the scheme. More that 70 percent of the non-members have never heard about the GHIP. One can only make a decision, when s/he knows what s/he can choose from. There is still much room to improve on the communication strategy. Those, who are familiar with the GHIP have received their information about the GHIP individually, through word-of-mouth by their neighbors or the Barangay health worker (> 65 percent). Only 28 percent were informed in organized meetings like village assemblies.

Difficulties in campaigning and distribution of information are the most important reasons why sustainability of the GHIP is jeopardized. Once somebody becomes a member, the possibility that the membership will not last long is high. The vast majority of respondents, who once subscribed to the GHIP, quit their membership because they missed the deadline of renewal. Since everybody has his or her individual deadline for paying the contribution, it is great challenge for the GHIP to remind each individual to pay the contribution for the next twelve months.

The improvement of the flow of information is one of the future challenges, which the GHIP has to meet, since more than 50 percent of the respondents simply forgot to renew their membership. However, improving the communication strategy is not the sole key to sustain and raise membership figures. The reasons why people do not join a health insurance are numerous such as the lack of information and financial resources, long distances to providers, poor quality of health care, high transaction costs or a poor benefit package.

8.1.3. GHIP's Contribution for Reducing Out-of-Pocket Spending

Those, who are members of a health insurance, assume that their health care expenses are covered in case of illness. If the insuree agreed to a ceiling, he or she should have knowledge on the costs of health care in general to estimate whether the ceiling is sufficient to cover cost intensive treatments and how much he or she would have to pay on an out-of-pocket basis. As pointed out earlier, most of the insurees choose the subsidized tariff of 85 pesos with a ceiling of 2500 pesos. The data in Table 23 shows that the benefit package offered by the GHIP is not sufficient to reduce the out-of-pocket payment. It was found that 67 percent of the insurees, who financed their cost for the treatment (with the help of the GHIP) had to pay more than 1500 pesos, while only 22 percent had to pay less than 500 pesos out of pocket during the last twelve months. Non-members pay less and seem to avoid expensive treatments. Thirty-three percent spent more than 1500 pesos while 52 percent spent less than 500.

It may be that membership in GHIP does not reduce the out-of pocket spending. On the other hand, it might paradoxically push for additional spending. Insurance members are encouraged to seek more expensive medical care when needed, but the low coverage of the GHIP cannot reduce the out-of-pocket payment effectively. The ceiling seems to be too low when staying in a hospital is longer than 24 hours. The main achievement of the GHIP seems to be that the insurees are aware of medical facilities and are willing to make use of them. However, the financial support of the scheme offers (in case of illness) is not sufficient. Since the GHIP has sufficient funds available, the benefit package could be extended in order to reduce the out-of -pocket spending and increase the low utilization rate of currently only 2.1 percent in 2000.

Table 23: Financing of Illness and Sum paid Out-of-Pocket During the last 12 Months

GHIP Member	Financing of illness			Sum Paid of Pocket					Total
				Less than 500 pesos	501-1000 pesos	1001-1500 pesos	more than 1500 pesos	don't know	
No	Out of pocket	No.		33	6	2	21	1	63
		%		52.4	9.5	3.2	33.3	1.6	100.0
	Total	No.		33	6	2	21	1	63
		%		52.4	9.5	3.2	33.3	1,6	100.0
Yes	Out of pocket	No.		44	11	11	12	3	81
		%		54.3	13.6	13.6	14.8	3,7	100.0
	GHIP and insuree	No.		4	1	1	12		18
		%		22.2	5.6	5.6	66.7		100.0
	Total	No.		48	12	12	24	3	99
		%		48.5	12.1	12.1	24.2	3.0	100.0

8.2. Willingness to Join the Raffle

The sample can be divided in terms of members and non-members of the GHIP. Both groups show a surprisingly high interest in joining the raffle. Majority (88.5 percent) of the member group want to join the raffle and only 11.5 percent answered that they are not sure or that they do not want to join. The results are similar in the non-member group. Majority (81.4 percent) want to join the raffle, while 18.6 percent do not want to join both the GHIP and the raffle or do not know, whether they want to join. The question arises why the respondents are so enthusiastic to join the raffle. Most of the respondents (Table24) of the Non-Member Group answered that the raffle offers a "better value for the money" (40 percent), while the majority of the Member-Group answered, "prizes increase my income" (45.3 percent).

Table 24: Reasons for joining the raffle in the GHIP

Reasons	NM join insurance and raffle	M join raffle and insurance
Better value for my money	40	29,5
I like gambling	0	1
The prices could help me to increase my income	35,8	45,3
The additional regulations are easy to fulfill	4,2	6,3
Other	20	17,9
Total	100	100

N= 190, in percent

As shown in Table 7 the raffle participants have the chance to win prices. The respondents were asked what kind of awards they would prefer. While designing the regulations, it was assumed that the target group would be most attracted by electronic devices. This is why the award electronic device was assigned to the "Gold Level" – the status that is most difficult to qualify for. However, the respondents have another preference – they prefer living poultry or livestock.

Figure 8: Preferred raffle prizes

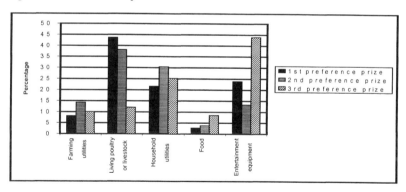

Figure 8 and table 24 show that a participation in the raffle and GHIP is not only a consideration of being protected against the risks of illness. The respondents take into account their general situation, living standard, and how the raffle prices could increase their income and food security. Prizes with a short-term benefit like food are not popular.

Food shortage is the main problem, which the respondents suffer most from (68 percent) after health (45 percent) (Table 25). With the participation of the raffle within the insurance, the respondents can cope with two major difficulties should they win a prize. First, they have protection against the financial risks of being ill due to the health insurance. Second, they have the chance to increase their income due to the prizes, and third, the prizes (livestock) have the function of a "savings account", which can be sold in times of uncertainties to overcome financial calamities. The suggested raffle model within the GHIP targets to the main challenges of the respondents, which could explain the tremendously high willingness of the respondents to join the raffle.

Table 25: Most Important Problems

	Most important problem	2nd important problem	3rd important problem	4th important problem	5th important problem
Food	**68**	12	8	3	8
Clothing	1	10	22	**46**	19
Health	14	**45**	26	9	6
Education	11	26	**29**	15	19
Housing	5	7	15	28	**49**
Total	100	100	100	100	100

N= 222, in percent.

8.3. Willingness to Pay for the Raffle

If a raffle scheme were to be introduced, contributions by households may rise due to expenses for raffle prizes and additional administration costs. Hence, a willingness to pay approach was used to assess how respondents estimated the value of the raffle and how much extra fee would be appropriate to charge for participation. The willingness to pay (WTP) analysis includes all households, which were willing to join the raffle, whether they were insurance members or not. In total, 195 households are covered in this analysis.

The participants of the survey were asked whether they would be willing to pay an extra fee for participating in the raffle. Those who were willing to pay, were asked how much they would be willing to pay. The current GHIP's subsidized minimum contribution is 85 pesos per year and household, which should be affordable for every household regarding the average annual income of 40,200 pesos. Therefore, it can be concluded that the ability to pay is given and that even a higher contribution is bearable.

First the respondents were asked whether they would pay an additional amount of 150 pesos in order to participate in the raffle. If not, they were asked whether they would be willing to contribute an additional fee of 75 pesos and so on. Those respondents, who were willing to pay the suggested amount, switched to the next section in the questionnaire. The following results indicate the readiness to pay for the raffle.

Table 26: Willingness to Pay for the Raffle

Additional payment	Number	Percent
None	11	6
20 pesos and less	5	3
40 pesos	66	34
75 pesos	36	18
150 pesos	77	39
Total	195	100

More than 92 percent were willing to pay an extra fee of at least 40 pesos per year in addition to the annual premium for the GHIP membership. Only six percent were not willing to pay a higher contribution.

The following ordinal regression analysis operated with SPSS 11.01 gives an oversight on the parameter estimators, which influence the WTP for the raffle model. The selection of the chosen variables is based on the assumption that the more financial resources a household has, the higher is the WTP and the spending capacity of the household for the raffle. Hence, the variables are directly or indirectly associated with the monthly available cash income, except for the variable age (AGEKAT). Table 23 on out of pocket spending during the last twelve months has shown that even insured households spend extra amount of money for health care. Illness is a cost-intensive event for both groups (insured and uninsured households) that reduces their available income significantly. Therefore, variables describing the health status were used in the WTP-analysis. First, the respondents were asked whether a household member suffered from a serious illness during the last twelve months (SUFFILLHH) and how long the individual on average had to stop his/her usual activities due to serious illness (DURA_HH). The latter variable represents the more severe cases of illness than the variable SUFFILL_HH, since DURA_HH sums up all days, where people were not able to perform their daily duties.

Furthermore, out-of-pocket spending stretches the monthly available income. The variable POCK500 includes all households, which have spent more than 500 pesos for health related expenses during the last twelve months. The variable "self-employed business men/women" (INCO_S2) classifies the group into the "poorest of the poor." This does not carry out any agricultural activities that would ease out their food consumption. In addition, the size of the household (HHSIZEKA) affects their wealth and the income per capita (NINCO_PC). Both variables were used in the following model. The following list gives an overview of the variables used for the ordinal regression analysis and their categorization:

- Average number of days that household members suffered from a serious illness and had to stop their usual activities (DURA_HH)
- Respondent achieved secondary school or college degree (EDUHIGH)
- Self-employed business men/women representing the most disadvantaged groups (INCO_S2)
- At least one household member suffered from a serious illness during the last twelve months (SUFFILLHH)
- Households with a out-of-pocket spending for health care with more than 500 pesos (POCK500)
- Income per capita in quartiles (NINCO_PC, 1=lowest quartile, 4=highest quartile)
- Household size categories (HHSIZEKA, 1 = 1-3, 2 = 4-6, 3= through highest),
- Age of the household head (AGEKAT, 1 = 15-30 year, 2 = 31 – 45 years, 3 = 46 – 60 years, 4 = 61 through highest years)

The analysis (table 27) shows, which variables are significant and how the respondents were affected by their willingness to pay for the raffle.

Table 27: Ordinal Regression: Willingness to Pay for the Raffle

Variable	Estimator	Standard Error
ADD_PAY = 0	-4,974	0,885
ADD_PAY = 1	-4,799	0,877
ADD_PAY = 2	-2,358	0,817
ADD_PAY = 3	-1,462	0,805
DURA_HH	-0,025**	0,011
EDUHIGH=0	-0,676**	0,329
INCO_S2=0	0,540	0,347
SUFILLHH=0	-0,856***	0,323
POCK500=0	0,527**	0,315
NINCO_PC=1	-1,372***	0,463
NINCO_PC=2	-0,742*	0,425
NINCO_PC=3	-0,870**	0,439
HHSIZEKA=1	-0,805	0,528
HHSIZEKA=2	-0,084	0,373
AGEKAT=1	-0,918	0,577
AGEKAT=2	-1,315***	0,521
AGEKAT=3	-0,814**	0,488
Logit estimation: *** Significance at 0.01% or better ** Significance at 0.05% or better * Significance of 0.1% or better Chi-square: 33.827*** R-square: 0.18 N = 195		

The model is highly significant and R Square is 18 percent. Those households that had to stop their daily duties due to illness are less willing to pay. The variable (SUFFILLHH) shows that healthier households who did not suffer from any serious illness are also less willing to spend extra for the raffle. Households who paid more than 500 pesos out of pocket (POCK500) are willing to pay more. A low per capita income (NINCO_PC) and a low education (EDUHIGH) reduce the respondents' willingness to pay for the raffle, while the older households (AGEKAT) would pay less as well. The household size does not affect the respondents' willingness to pay.

8.4 Determinants to Participate in the Raffle within the GHIP

8.4.1. Variables Influencing the Likelihood to Join the Raffle

The following models are based on determinants for participation in local organizations. They include a variable stating the health status of the household, which could influence the respondents' willingness to participate in a community-based health insurance (CBHI) with or without raffle option. The estimation is based on the sample of 226 households. Different models are suggested with the same variables, but with different sample sizes. An add-and-drop approach was applied. The equation below was used both for members and non-members of the insurance. It is assumed that participation (P) in local organizations, such as CBHI, is a function of different characteristics. Those characteristics influence the decision-making progress and determine the likelihood of the respondents' joining in the raffle. The variable Z_{hh} represents the household characteristics (Z_{hh}), while the monthly per capita income of the household is represented by (Y), and, lastly, the health status (H_{hh}) of the household members. With these variables participation in a CBHI can be determined as:

$$P = f(Z_{hh}, Y, H_{hh})$$

The variable used to represent the household characteristics is Z_{hh}. It is assumed that the household size *(HH_SIZE)* influences the willingness to join the raffle. Since the cost-benefit ratio for larger households are more advantageous than for smaller households (due to the free membership of dependants in the GHIP), the sign of this variable is expected to be positive.

It is hypothesized that the age *(AGE)* of the household head is one important indicator, which correlates strongly with the willingness of the respondents to join the raffle. It is assumed that younger household heads are more open-minded to innovative approaches such as insurance or the suggested raffle model than older household heads. Therefore, a negative sign is expected. Further, it is assumed that the duration of education influences the respondents' likelihood to join the raffle.

The variable level of education (*EDUHIGH*) includes those household heads with secondary and college education. It is presumed that their likelihood to participate rises with the obtained degree, since they are more likely to understand fully the complex details of the insurance and the raffle regulations. Therefore, a positive sign is expected. Variables, describing the characteristics of the respondent, i.e. sex, etc. were not taken into further consideration in the following models. It is assumed that while making the hypothetical decision on whether to participate or not, the holistic situation of the family was taken into account since the decision affects all family members. Nevertheless, the age and the education can be regarded as individual characteristics, but the data show a strong relationship of the age and education of the respondents with their spouses. Young respondents have young spouses; better-educated respondents have better educated partners with a strong effect to the family as a whole. This assumption allows generalizing these individual characteristics to the household level. The variables age (*AGE*) and level of education (*EDUHIGH*) are therefore regarded as household characteristics.

It is obvious, the source of income has a direct impact on the respondents' monthly available cash. In the context of Guimaras, income alone is not a suitable indicator to identify the poor. Small-scale farmers might have a very low monthly income, but they are able to grow sufficient food for their own consumption. Even if they belong to the group of the poor, food security for farmers is better than for vendors or small-scale business men/women, who generate their income solely with trading. These businessmen/women do not practice any agricultural activities and have to spend a considerable amount of money on food, which even stretches their small monthly budget. Due to this distinction between these two low-income groups, the assumed poorer group of street vendors and small shop owners were chosen to identify the poorest of the poor. The poor street vendors and shop-owners are bundled in the variable *INCO_S2*. It is proposed that these low-income families tend not join the GHIP or the raffle due to lack of money and therefore, the expected sign is negative

To explain the income (*Y*) the self-reported income per capita (*INCO_PC*) was used with the assumption that the higher the income per capita, the higher is the respondents' willingness to join the insurance and raffle. They also have higher opportunity costs in case of illness. Besides, income is often related to the educational degree and, as mentioned above, it is assumed that educated households are more likely to understand the insurance principle. Consequently, it is predicted that sign is positive.[1]

Furthermore, the variable describing whether at least one household member suffered from a serious illness during the last twelve months *(SUFFILLHH)* was used to describe the health status of the household *(H_{hh})*. A more detailed description on the problem of measuring illness and the definition of the variable *SUFFILLHH* is given above. It is hypothesized that those households, who suffered from a serious illness would not tend to join the raffle but the insurance, since the experience of being sick would put the focus more on the benefits of the health insurance than additional features like a raffle.

The following binary Logit analysis was undertaken with SPSS 11.01. The R^2 for Probit and Logit estimations are based on the log likelihood. Thus, the R^2 in the following models is generally lower than in ordinary least square estimations. Table 28 visualizes the different variables used, the sample groups, and the expected results:

Table 28: Overview of Variables Used with the Expected Outcome

Variable	Description	Expected sign			
		Join GHIP all	Join raffle within GHIP/ all	Join raffle within GHIP/ member	Join raffle within GHIP/ non-member
AGE	Age of the household head	(-)	(-)	(-)	(-)
HH_SIZE	Size of the household	(+)	(+)	(+)	(+)
INCO_PC	Per capita income	(+)	(+)	(+)	(+)
INCO_S2	Main income source: self-employed business man	(-)	(-)	(-)	(-)
SUFILLHH	Suffered from serious illness during the last twelve months	(+)	(-)	(-)	(-)
EDUHIGH	Attended higher education, secondary school and college	(+)	(+)	(+)	(+)

---

1   Both variables *INCO_PC* and *INCO_S2* are related to the self-reported income. Every analysis has to face the problem of accuracy and trustworthiness of the collected data of the income. This study is no exception, however, tendency can be demonstrated.

Firstly, the whole sample was studied in detail. The members and non-members of the sample were analyzed to see whether the chosen variables showed any significance concerning the likelihood of joining the GHIP without the raffle option. In a second step, based on the whole sample, the probability of joining the raffle within the insurance was estimated. Thirdly, the sample was divided into non-members and members. In both groups, estimation on the likelihood of joining the raffle within the insurance was undertaken.

8.4.2. Model 1: Determinants for Joining the Insurance: Members and Non-Members

With the Logit analysis, there is no proof of the significance of the chosen determinants. None of the characteristics raise the likelihood of joining the GHIP as it can be seen in table 29. This means that the characteristics of the GHIP membership are similar to those of the non-member group. This leads to the conclusion that the health status, income, level of education and the household size show no differences to the non-members. On the other hand, the GHIP members represent the average of the sample. It could therefore be deduced that no risk selection is given and that the current membership structure of the GHIP represents the average characteristics of the whole sample.

Table 29: Determinants for Joining the GHIP: Members and Non-Members

Variable	Coefficient	Standard Error
AGE	0.003	0.011
HH_SIZE	0.119	0.070
INCO_PC	0.00008	0.0002
INCO_S2	0.262	0.325
SUFILLHH	0.466	0.280
EDUHIGH	0.230	0.311
Constant	-1.137	0.812
Logit estimation: *** Significance at 0.01% or better ** Significance at 0.05% or better * Significance of 0.1% or better Chi-squared: 6.686 R-squared: 0.039 N= 224		

8.4.3. Model 2: Determinants for Joining the Raffle: Members and Non-Members

As outlined in chapter 4, the raffle model suggests that individuals have the option to join the raffle within the framework of the insurance. The respondents were asked whether they want to join the raffle or not. The following estimation analyzes the determinants of joining the raffle of members as well as non-members. R^2 has a value of 9 percent, but the statistic significance level of the overall model is high (< 0,01). The variables age *(AGE)*, household size *(HH_SIZE)*, income per capita *(INCO_PC)*, and low-income household *(INCO_S2)* show a significance, while the health status *(SUFILLHH)* and the level of education *(EDUHIGH)* are not.

Results show that the younger the household head, [variable *(AGE)*], the higher the likelihood that the respondents will join the raffle. The bigger the household is, the higher the probability that they will also join the raffle. Older household heads seem not to be attracted by the raffle as much as younger households. A reason for higher participation probabilities of younger households could be explained that it would be easier for them to qualify for the raffle. Another is to fulfill the required participation in health education programs and actively promote the insurance so as to convince uninsured households to join the GHIP. Those tasks are probably easier to achieve by the younger generation.

Table 30: Determinants for Joining the Raffle: Members and Non-Members

Variable	Coefficient	Standard Error
AGE	-0.038**	0.017
HH_SIZE	0.237**	0.114
INCO_PC	0.001**	0.0004
INCO_S2	-1.140**	0.472
SUFILLHH	0.181	0.423
EDUHIGH	0.289	0.495
Constant	2.027	1.319
Logit estimation: *** Significance at 0.01% or better ** Significance at 0.05% or better * Significance of 0.1% or better Chi-squared: 20.194*** R-squared: 0.159 N= 223		

The household size *(HH_SIZE)* has a positive impact on participation in the suggested raffle. The analysis shows that households with many dependents are more interested in participating in the raffle compared to households with less dependents. At first glance, the correlation between household size and the willingness of the respondents to participate in the raffle is not obvious. However, household heads with many dependents are usually younger. Older household heads might have many grown-up dependents as well, which are not recorded in this survey, since household members are generally defined in this survey based on the GHIP requirement for free insurance coverage[16]. This might explain the correlation between household size and the willingness of the respondents to join the raffle due to the fact that the household size according to the GHIP definition correlates strongly with age. The relationship between age *(AGE)* and raffle participation has already been explained.

As mentioned above it is assumed that the financial status of the household influences the decision whether to join the raffle or not. The analysis supports the assumption that the higher the income per capita *(INCO_PC)*, the higher the likelihood that the respondent will join the raffle and, vice versa – e.g., low income groups such as street vendors *(INCO_S2)*, are less willing to join the raffle.

To meet the requirements to join the raffle, time intensive work for the insurance or participation in health courses is necessary. It can be speculated, whether the "poorest of the poor" on the one hand have no time to fulfill the prerequisites to join or are just not interested in joining since they might have more pressing concerns. Better off households, on the other hand, are willing to spend additional time to qualify for the raffle.

The health status or the educational level of the respondents show no significance and have no bearing in their joining the raffle. In general, these results show that the better off and younger households are more attracted to the raffle, while the poorer households and those households with older heads seem not to be interested in joining raffle.

8.4.4. Model 3: Determinants for Joining the Raffle: Non-Members

The following model (table 31) includes only the non-members of this survey. This sample group did not only make the decision on whether they would like to join the insurance, but also whether they want to join the raffle as well. The R2 (14 percent) has improved compared to the previous model. The overall significance of the model is very good with 0.0103 percent. In this model, the same variables were used as in the previous models and three out of seven variables show significance, whose interpretation has to include possible thoughts

---

16   Dependents older than 21 years or living already in an own household have to pay their
      own insurance premium.

of the decision-maker on a possible GHIP membership and raffle participation as well. The variables household size (HH_SIZE), self-employed businessmen/women (INCO_S2) and the health status (SUFFILLHH) has been found to be significant.

Table 31: Determinants for Joining the Insurance and the Raffle: Non-Members

Variable	Coefficient	Standard Error
AGE	-0.031	0.024
HH_SIZE	0.308*	0.176
INCO_PC	0.0007	0.0005
INCO_S2	-1.355**	0.694
SUFILLHH	1.232*	0.666
EDUHIGH	0.944	0.720
Constant	0.855	1.837
Logit estimation: *** Significance at 0.01% or better ** Significance at 0.05% or better * Significance of 0.1% or better Chi-squared: 16.729*** R-squared: 0.247 N= 108		

The significance of the variable household size *(HH_SIZE)* can be explained through the fact that dependents are insured for free under the GHIP. Additionally, households with many dependents tend to be younger, which are supposed to be more open to innovative approaches such as a raffle combined with a health insurance. The variable age *(AGE)* as in the previous model, however, shows no significance. In this model, as also observed in the foregoing models, low-income groups *(INCO_S2)* tend not to join the raffle within the insurance. The raffle does not have the elements to attract the poorest households for them to be able to want to become a member of the GHIP.

The health status of the non-members *(SUFFILLHH)* is a significant variable that the respondents consider in joining the raffle within the framework of insurance. Households, who got sick during the last twelve months, are more likely to participate than the healthy households. The result is probably mainly based on the attractiveness of the insurance and not on the raffle. But once the decision was made to join the insurance, the raffle option was chosen as well. They prefer to choose the "package" of insurance combined with the raffle. The level of education *(EDUHIGH)* seems not to influence the decision on participation. No significance could be proven.

8.4.5. Model 4: Determinants for Joining the Raffle: Members

This model includes only the subgroup 'members of the insurance' to determine their likelihood to join the raffle. The R^2 is acceptable with eleven percent and a good significance of the model in its entirety with a significance level of 0.03 percent. Three variables show significance: Age *(AGE)*, business men/women *(INCOME_S2)*, and those who suffered from a serious illness *(SUFFILLHH)*.

Table 32: Determinants for Joining the Insurance and the Raffle: Members

Variable	Coefficient	Standard Error
AGE	-0.058**	0.030
HH_SIZE	0.156	0.171
INCO_PC	0.002	0.001
INCO_S2	-1.256*	0.737
SUFILLHH	-1.208*	0.738
EDUHIGH	-0.555	0.736
Constant	4.307*	2.345
Logit estimation: *** Significance at 0.01% or better ** Significance at 0.05% or better * Significance of 0.1% or better Chi-squared: 13.879** R-squared: 0.225 N= 115		

As observed in the previous models, the younger the household *(AGE)* the more the respondents are attracted by the raffle option and their willingness to participate. On the other hand, small-scale traders *(INCO_S2)* have a lower probability to join the raffle. Households with family members who were ill during the last twelve months *(SUFFILLHH)* are likely to be averse to join the raffle. They seem to be contented with the existing insurance features or worry more on their health status than joining the proposed raffle. The level of education has no influence to their likelihood to join the raffle.

9. Summary and Conclusion

9.1. Summary of Main Findings

Risk management tools for the poor are a key element for sustainable development. Comprehensive risk management enhances well-being, reduces vulnerability, improves consumption smoothing and increases equity. This results in economic development and growth, since smoothed consumption encourages households to engage in high-risk and high-yielding activities and improves effectiveness. Additionally, protection against risks reduces transitory poverty and prevents that poor people fall deeper in poverty. It thus provides an instrument to overcome poverty.

Community-based health insurance schemes are an important tool to secure the poor against the risk of illness. They mobilize financial resources that can be spent for health care delivery and they improve the health status. They contribute to a more effective and efficient health care provision, since contracts with providers lead to a greater accountability in terms of monitoring the costs and quality of care. Further, contracts can specify what kind of health care is provided and therefore the provider can concentrate on offering the contracted health care cost-efficiently. This has the effect that clients demand improved health care, because they can understand the quality of health care with the payment of their health insurance premiums, while competition among providers increases efficiency and effectiveness.

However, low coverage and high drop out rates lead to adverse selection jeopardizing the financial stability of CBHI. To improve the risk profile of the CBHI "good risks" have to join the insurance to improve risk sharing. Additional incentives to attract new members and to reduce the drop out rates are required. A raffle model as an incentive to join the insurance was therefore suggested to members and non-members of a CBHI in the Philippines. The following rules were proposed: Each insurance number could have the function of a lot. Every paying member, upon passing the qualification requirement, would have the opportunity to join the raffle. Qualifying, in general, means the acceptance of additional regulations, i.e. the recruitment of two new GHIP members annually. The raffle participant could join the raffle at different levels depending on the regulation he or she is willing to join. The value of the award would rise simultaneously with the stage at which the insuree has qualified for. In brief: The higher the stage, the harder the regulation and the harder the regulation, the higher is the value of the possible awards. The participation in the raffle would be voluntary for insurance members. Households, who are not a member of the CBHI, would have to join the insurance, before they can join the raffle.

After introducing the raffle scheme to members and non-members both, a survey was carried out among households, to determine willingness to participate and their willingness to pay for the raffle approach, covering 226 households (115 member households and 111 non-member households) The most important results of the survey were:

- The vast majority of the respondents wants to join the raffle within the insurance.
- The respondents would accept higher premiums to join the raffle.
- Raffle prizes that can improve the household's income are preferred.
- Younger and larger households with a higher per capita income are more interested in joining the raffle than older, smaller and poorer households.
- Health status did not affect the decision of the respondents, thus no risk selection could be observed.

The suggested raffle model attracts new members. Almost 90 percent of the GHIP member group and more than 80 percent of the non-member group would like to join the raffle. On average, they are willing to accept an increase of the premium by almost 50 percent (an additional raise of 40 pesos from the current 85 pesos premium). The respondents are both: risk-averse and risk-seeking. They are risks-averse in respect to negative changes to their current wealth level due to sickness. On the other hand, they are risk-seeking in respect to prospects that improve their social status significantly. Therefore, they are willing to join the raffle.

Joining the raffle in the GHIP provides more benefits to the target group. In addition to the protection against the financial burden of illness, they can experience the excitement of joining a game of chance. Winning prices such as farming utilities can help to improve the household's income.

The results indicate that younger and larger households with a higher per capita income are more attracted by the raffle than the very poor households. However, the latter are less interested to join the insurance without the raffle option as well. Regarding the health status, the results do not indicate that healthier households are more interested in joining the raffle. Households, who have members that have experience of being sick are just as interested to participate. Additionally, households with many children would like to join. Based on these results it can be concluded that a CBHI combined with a raffle would not lead to risk selection.

9.2. Lessons Learned and Policy Implications

Whether CBHI will be successful in a long run and be able to operate sustainable without major subsidies from external sources depend on the awareness of several actors on the micro and macro level of their role and responsibility in fostering CBHI in developing countries. A first step would be to provide these schemes a strong regulatory framework. The framework can also secure a formal accreditation process and ensure supervision of CBHI. However, this requires well-developed and strong institutions that have the capacity to monitor the operations of CBHI from an independent point of view. In addition, innovative approaches such as government-run re-insurance for CBHI could provide protection against large expenditure fluctuations.

Another key policy instrument to stabilize CBHI to improve the effectiveness and sustainability could be an increase of governmental subsidies on health expenditures and to contribute a substantial share of these subsidies for premium payment of low-income groups and the provision of health care. However, research has shown, including this analysis, that the poorest of the poor can often not be reached even with subsidized premiums and the inclusion of this group can only be realized with their social empowerment.

Further, the set up of CBHI`s umbrella organizations could provide technical support during the design and implementation and provide assistance in running a health insurance. Those umbrella organizations could also advocate CBHI's interest towards government institutions and develop joint marketing campaigns to increase membership figures.

Regarding the implementation of the raffle the main task would be to strengthen the administrative capacity such as professional accounting procedures and membership administration. Accurate membership figures are required as well as sound reporting structures, to determine whether a household qualifies to join the raffle. Additionally, the implementation should be accompanied by a marketing campaign to inform the target group about the new feature. To fulfill these prerequisites, external support by donor agencies or NGOs is required, despite the fact that the target group would accept a raise of premiums to join the raffle. Training in accounting, bookkeeping, computer-based membership administration and marketing are necessary to succeed with the raffle implementation. Depending on the size of the CBHI, it is estimated that it can take up to one year to prepare a CBHI for the introduction of the raffle scheme.

The success of the raffle model and CBHI in general depends on various factors such as:

- stable political conditions and supporting government action such as financial support and clear policy framework
- an analysis of the demand for the raffle within the CBHI including a willingness and ability to pay analysis
- community participation and "ownership" by clients
- promotion of partnership with providers and government units on health care provision
- sufficient financial support from governments or NGOs
- implementation of instruments to avoid adverse selection, moral hazard and supplier induced demand tailored to the local conditions.
- sound management capacities including marketing by CBHI's staff
- sound product design and training of the management before setting up a CBHI combined with a raffle

9.3 Future Research Needs

Research on social security and particularly health care financing has a long tradition. Regarding CBHI, much research has been conducted during the last decade in respect to performance measuring of CBHI, classification of CBHI and their impact on health seeking behavior and health care delivery in rural areas in developing countries. Most of the literature point at the problems CBHIs have to face and refer to solutions on the micro level, but mostly on the meso and macro level, which are usually more difficult to put into practice.

During the phase of defining the degree of social protection in developing countries and the tools to achieve the goals in a country, innovative ways of social risk management and tools have to be invented. The developing world building up systems of social risk management has the opportunity to learn from previous successes made in developed countries, but also trying to avoid aberrations that occurred in developed countries. Future research on health care financing should be more imaginative in order to detect innovative instruments for social security systems in developing countries. To identify the most appropriate approaches in different cultural and socio-economic settings the knowledge and scientific tools of various disciplines such as political science, medicine, economics, sociology, and anthropology have to be brought together. However, each innovative intervention on health care financing should undergo a feasibility study and should be monitored thoroughly to ensure cost control of the activities. An impact assessment will provide additional information of the success but also limits of the intervention.

This study has shown that the raffle model is a promising approach to improve the coverage and risk sharing of CBHI. However, whether the model will be successful has to be tested by implementing this model in a CBHI. The Deutsche Gesellschaft für Technische Zusammenarbeit (GTZ) plans to implement the model in the GHIP, where the survey took place. The process execution should be accompanied scientifically to discover weak points and strengths of the new approach. A cost-benefit evaluation should take place regularly to measure the performance of the scheme and how the raffle affects the basic indicators of the scheme. The future will show whether the raffle model will have the anticipated impacts on coverage and risk sharing.

10. References

ADAMS, D. AND CANAVESI DE SAHONERO, M., (1989). Rotating Savings and Credit Associations in Bolivia, Savings and Development Quarterly Review, Vol. 13, No. 3., 219-236.

AGARWAL, B., (1991). Social Security and the Family: Coping with Seasonality and Calamity in Rural India, in: Ahmad, E.; Drèze, J.; Hills, J.; Sen, A. (Ed.), Social Security in Developing Countries, Oxford, pp. 171- 246.

ALCHIAN, A. AND DEMSETZ, H. (1972). Production, Information Costs, and Economic Organization, American Economic Review, Vol. 62, pp. 777 – 795.

ASENO-OKYERE, K. W., OSEI-AKOTO, I., ANUM, A. AND APPIAH, E, (1997). Willingness to Pay for Health Insurance in a Developing Economy: A Pilot Study of the Informal Sector of Ghana Using Contingent Valuation, Health Policy, Vol. 42, pp. 223-237.

ASFAW, A., (2002). Cost of Illness, Demand for Medical Care and the Prospect of Community Health Insurance Schemes in the Rural Areas of Ethiopia, Dissertation, University of Bonn, Bonn.

ASIAN DEVELOPMENT BANK (2001). Country Strategy and Program Update, Manila.

_____(2002). Key Indicators of Developing Asian and Pacific Countries, Manila.

ATIM, C. (1998). Contribution of Mutual Health Organizations to Financing, Delivery, and Access to Health Care, Synthesis of Research in Nine West and Central-African Countries. Technical Report No. 18. Bethesda, MD. Partnership for Health Reform Projects. Abt Asociates.

_____(1999). Social Movements and Health Insurance: a Critical Evaluation of Voluntary, Non-Profit Insurance Schemes with Case Studies from Ghana and Cameroon, Social and Science Medicine, Vol. 48, p. 881-896.

AXELROD, R. (1984). The Evolution of Cooperation, 1984.

BALKENHOL, B. AND CHURCHILL, C. (2002) From Micro-insurance to Micro-Health Insurance, In: Dror, D. and Preker, AS., Eds. Social Reinsurance: A New Approach to Sustainable Community Health Financing, World Bank/ILO.

BECKER, G. S. (1973). A Theory of Marriage: Part 1, Journal of Political Economy, Vol. 81, July/August, pp. 813-846.

_____(1974). A Theory of Marriage: Part 2, Journal of Political Economy, Vol. 82, No. 2, pp. S11-S26.

BECKER, L. (1990). Reciprocity, Chicago.

BECKER, S. W. AND BROWNSON, F. O. (1964). What Price Ambiguity? Or the Role of Ambiguity in Decision Making, Journal of Political Economy, Vol. 72, pp.62 – 73.

BELLI, P. (2001). How Adverse Selection Affects the Health Insurance Market, Policy Research Working Paper No. 2574, Development Research Group Public Economics, The World Bank, Washington.

BENNETT, S., CREESE,A. AND MONASCH, R. (1998). Health Insurance Schemes for People Outside Formal Sector Employment, ARA Paper No. 6, WHO, Geneva.

BENNETT, S. AND GILSON, L. (2001). Health Financing: Designing and Implementing Pro-Poor Policies, Health System Resource Center, DFID, London.

BENNET, S. AND GOTSADZE, G. (2002). Building Capacity and Strengthening Implementation at the Community Level, in: Dror, D. and Preker, A. S., Eds. Social Reinsurance: A New Approach to Sustainable Community Health Financing, World Bank/ILO, Washington, Geneva.

BLOOM, D. E., CANNING, D. AND SEVILLA, J. (2001). The Effect of Health on Economic Growth: Theory and Evidence, NBER Working Paper Series, WP 8587.3.13.03, Cambridge, MA.

BLOOM, G. AND SHENGLAN, T. (1999). Rural Health Prepayment Schemes in China: Towards a More Active Role for Government, Social Science and Medicine, Vol. 48, pp. 951-960.

BHATTACHARYA, P. C. (2000). An Analysis of Rural-to-Rural Migration in India, Journal of International Development, Vol. 12, No. 5, pp. 655-667.

BINSWANGER, H. P. (1981). Attitudes Towards Risk: Theoretical Implications of an Experiment in Rural India, The Economic Journal, Vol. 91, pp. 867-890.

BOUMAN, F. (1977). Indigenous Savings and Credit Associations in the Third World, A Message, Savings and Development, Vol. 1, No. 4, 181-214.

BOYD, R. AND RICHERSON, P. (1988). The Evolution of Reciprocity in Sizable Groups, Journal of Theoretical Biology 132 (June), pp. 337-356.

_____(1992), Punishment Allows the Evolution of Cooperation (or anything else) in Sizeable Groups, Ethnology and Sociobiology, May, pp. 171-195.

BROWN, W. AND CHURCHILL, C. F. (1999). Providing Insurance in Low-Income Countries, Part I: A Primer on Insurance Principles and Products, Microenterprise Best Practice, Bethesda, MD.

_____(2000). Insurance Provision in Low-Income Countries, Part II: Initial Lessons from Micro-Insurance for the Poor, Microenterprise Best Practice, Bethesda, MD.

BUCKLEY, G. (1997). Microfinance in Africa: Is it Either the Problem or the Solution?, World Development, Vol. 25, No. 7, pp. 1081-1093.

CALOMIRIS, C. W. AND RAJAMARAN, I. (1998). The Role of RoSCAs: Lumpy Durables or Event Insurance?, Journal of Development Economics, Vol. 56, p. 207-216.

COATE, S. AND RAVALLION, M. (1993). Reciprocity without Commitment: Characterization and Performance of Informal Insurance Arrangements, Journal of Development Economics, Vol. 40, pp.1-24.

COHEN, M., JAFFREY, J.Y AND SAID, T. (1985). Individual Behavior under Risk and under Uncertainty: An Experimental Study, Theory and Decision, Vol. 18, pp. 203 – 228.

COLLIER, P. AND GUNNING, J. W. (1999). Explaining African Economic Performance, Journal of Economic Literature, Vol. 37, No. 1, pp. 64-111.

CONN, C.P. AND WALFORD, V. (1998). An Introduction to Health Insurance for Low-Income Countries, Health System Resource Center, DFID, London.

CONNING, J. (1999). Outreach, Sustainability and Leverage in Monitored and Peer-Monitored Lending, Journal of Development Economics, Vol. 60, pp. 51-77.

COOK, K. AND M. LEVI (1990). The Limits of Rationality, Chicago.

CRIEL, B., VAN DER STUYFT, P. AND VAN LERBERGHE W. (1999). The Bwamanda Hospital Insurance Scheme: Effective for Whom? A Study of Impact on Hospitalization Utilization Patterns, Social Science and Medicine, Vol. 48, pp. 897-911.

CUTLER, D. M. AND ZECKHAUSER, R (1999). The Anatomy of Health Insurance, NBER Working Paper Series, WP 7176. Cambridge, MA.

DEATON, A. (1992). Understanding Consumption, Oxford.

DEPARTMENT OF HEALTH (2003). http://www.doh.gov.ph, Manila, Philippines.

DERCON, S. (2002). Income Risk, Coping Strategies and Safety Nets, Discussion Paper No. 2002/22, World Institute for Development Economics Research (UNU/WIDER), Helsinki.

_____(1996). Risk, Crop Choice and Savings: Evidence from Tanzania, Economic Development and Cultural Change, Vol. 94, No. 2, pp. 253-273.

DERCON, S. AND KRISHNAN, P. (1996). Income Portfolios in Rural Ethiopia and Tanzania: Choices and Constraints, Journal of Development Studies, Vol. 32, No. 6, pp. 850-875.

DESMET, M., CHOWDRY, A.Q. AND ISLAM, MD. K. (1999). The Potential for Social Mobilisation in Bangladesh: The Organisation and Functioning of Two Health Insurance Schemes, Social Science and Medicine, Vol. 48, pp. 925 - 938

DE WEERDT, J. (2002). Risk-Sharing and Endogenous Network Formation, Discussion Paper No. 2002/57, World Institute for Development Economics Research (UNU/WIDER), Helsinki.

DI MAURO, C., AND MAFFIOLETTI, A. (2001). The Valuation of Insurance under Uncertainty: Does Information about Probability Matter? The Geneva Papers on Risk and Insurance Theory, Vol. 26, pp. 195-224.

DROR, D. AND PREKER, AS., EDS. (2001). Social Re-Insurance: Improved Risks Sharing for Low-Income and Excluded Groups. Washington: World Bank/ILO.

EDNEY, J. (1979), Free Riders en Route to Disaster, Psychology Today, Vol. 13, pp. 80-102.

EINHORN, H. J., AND HOGHARTH, R. M. (1986). Decision Making under Ambiguity, Journal of Business, Vol 59, No. 4, pp. 225-250.

ELLSBERG, D. (1961). Risk, Ambiguity, and the Savage Axioms, Quarterly Journal of Economics, Vol. 75, pp. 643 – 669.

ESWARAN, M. AND KOTWAL, A. (1989). Credit as Insurance in Agrarian Economies, Journal of Development Economics, Vol. 31, No. 1, pp. 37-53.

FALK, A. AND FISCHBACHER, U. (2000). A Theory of Reciprocity, Working Paper, University of Zurich, Zurich.

FAFCHAMPS, M. (1999). Risk-Sharing and Quasi-Credit, Journal of International Trade and Economic Development, Vol. 3, No. 3, pp. 257-278.

FAFCHAMPS, M. AND LUND, S. (2001). Risk-Sharing Networks in Rural Philippines, Discussion Paper, University of Oxford, Dept. of Economics, Oxford.

FEHR, E. AND GÄCHTER, S. (2002). Do Incentive Contracts Undermine Voluntary Cooperation?, Working Paper 42, University of Zurich.

_____(2000). Fairness and Retaliation: The Economics of Reciprocity, Journal of Economic Perspectives 14, pp. 159-181.

FEHR, E. AND SCHMIDT, K. (1999). A Theory of Fairness, Competition and Cooperation, *Quarterly Journal of Economics* 114, pp. 817-868.

FEHR, E. AND SCHMIDT, K. (2001), Theories of Fairness and Reciprocity, Evidence and Economic Applications, Discussion Paper, Department of Economics, University of Munich.

FIEBIG, M., HANNIG, A. AND WISNIWSKI, S. (1999). Savings in the Context of Microfinance – State of Knowledge, Consultative Group to Assist the Poorest (CGAP), Working Group on Savings and Mobilization, Eschborn.

FOX, C. AND TVERSKY, A. (1995). Ambiguity Aversion and Comparative Ignorance, The Quarterly Journal of Economics, Vol. 10, pp. 585-603.

FRIEDMAN, M. AND SAVAGE, L.J. (1948). The Utility Analysis of Choices Involving Risk, Journal of Political Economy, Vol. 56, p. 279 – 304.

GARRET, T. AND SOBEL, R. (1999). Gamblers favor Skewness, not Risk: Further Evidence from United States' Lottery Games. Economic Letter, Vol. 63, pp. 85 – 90.

GEDDES, B. (1994). Politician's dilemma: Building state capacity in Latin America, Berkely.

GERTLER, P., LEVINE, D.I. AND MORETTI, E. (2003). Do Microfinance Programs Help Families Insure Consumption Against Illness? Paper 103-129, Center for International and Development Economics Research CIDER, University of California, Berkeley.

GILSON, L., KALYALYA, D., KUCHLER, F., LAKE, S., ORANGA, H. AND OUENDO, M. (2001). Strategies for Promoting Equity: Experience with Community Financing in Three African Countries, Health Policy, Vol. 58, pp. 37-67.

GOETZ, A. M. AND GUPTA, R. S. (1996). Who Takes the Credit? Gender, Power, and Control Over Loan Use in Rural Credit Programs in Bangladesh, World Development, Vol. 24, No. 1, pp. 45-63.

GOLEC, J. AND TAMARKI, M. (1998). Bettors Love Skewness, not Risks, at the Horse Track. Journal of Political Economy, Vol. 106, pp. 205 – 225.

GRIMARD, F. (1997). Household Consumption Smoothing through Ethnic ties: Evidence from Cote d'Ivoire, Journal of Development Economics, Vol. 53, pp. 391-422.

GROSSMAN, S. AND HART, O. (1980). Takeover Bids, the Free-Rider Problem, and the Theory of Cooperation, Bell Journal of Economics, Vol. 11, pp. 232-344.

GUETH, W. AND YAARI, M. (1992). An Evolutionary Approach to Explaining Reciprocal Behavior in a Simple Strategic Game. In: Explaining Process and Change. Approaches to Evolutionary Economics, Ed. Witt, Ulrich; Arbor, Ann, University of Michigan Press, pp. 23-34.

HOGARTH, R. M. AND KUNREUTHER, H. (1989). Risk, Ambiguity, and Insurance, Journal of Risk and Uncertainty, Vol. 2, pp. 5 – 35.

HOLSTROM, B. (1982). Moral Hazard in Teams, Bell Journal of Economics, Vol. 13 pp. 324 – 340.

HOLZMANN, R. AND JØRGENSEN, S. (2000). Social Risk Management: A Conceptual Framework for Social Protection and Beyond, Social Protection Discussion Paper No. 6, World Bank, Washington.

HSIO, W.C. (2001). Unmet Health Needs of Two Billion: Is Community Financing a Solution?, Background Paper No. 6 for the Commission of Macroeconomics and Health.

HULME, D. AND MOSLEY, P. (1996). Finance Against Poverty, London.

INTEGRATED COMMUNITY HEALTH SERVICE PROJECT (2002). Guimaras Health Insurance Program – A Model in Health Care Financing, Health Beat, Department of Health, Philippines, No. 35, pp. 25-28.

JACOBY , J. G. AND SKOUFIAS, E. (1997). Risk, Financial Markets and Human Capital in a Developing Country, Review of Economic Studies, Vol. 64, pp. 311-335.

JAKAB, M. AND KRISHNAN, C. (2001). Community Involvement in Health Care Financing: Impact, Strength and Weakness, A Synthesis of Literature, Backround Paper No. 9 for the Commission of Macroeconomics and Health.

JALAN, J. AND RAVAILLON, M. (1998). Transient Poverty in Postreform China. Journal of Comparative Economics, 26, pp. 338-357.

JÜTTING, J. (2000). Social Security Systems in Low-Income Countries: Concepts, Constraints and the Need for Cooperation. International Social Security Review, 53 (4), pp. 3 - 25.

_____(2002). Social Risk Management in Developing Countries. An Economic Analysis of Community-based Health Insurance Schemes. Monograph and "Habilitation Thesis", University of Bonn, Germany.

KAHNEMANN, D. AND TVERSKY, A. (1979). Prospect Theory: An Analysis of Decision Under Risk, Econometrica, Vol.47, No. 2, pp. 263 – 291.

KEYNES, J. M. (1957). A Treatise on Probability, London.

KIMBALL, M.S. (1988). Farmer's Cooperatives as Behavior Toward Risk, American Economic Revue, Vol. 78, No. 1, pp. 224-232.

KNIGHT, F. (1921). Risk, Uncertainty, and Profit, Boston.

KOCHERLAKOTA, N. R. (1996). Efficient Bilateral Risk Sharing without Commitment, Review of Economic Studies, Vol. 63, No. 4, pp. 594-606.

KOCHNAR, A. (1999). Smoothing Consumption by Smoothing Income: Hours-Of-Work Response to Idiosyncratic Agricultural Shocks in Rural India, The Review of Economics and Statistics, Vol. 81, No. 1, pp. 50-61.

KOTLIKOFF, L. AND SPIVAK, A. (1981). The Family as an Incomplete Annuities Market, Journal of Political Economy, Vol. 89, No.2, pp. 372-391.

LEVINSON, A. R. AND BESLEY, T. (1996). The Anatomy of an Informal Financial Market: RoSCA Participation in Taiwan, Journal of Development Economics, Vol. 51, pp. 45-68.

MARIAM, D. H. (2003). Indigenous Social Insurance as an Alternative Financing Mechanism for Health Care in Ethiopia (The Case of Eders), Social Science and Medicine, Vol. 56, No. 8, pp. 1719 – 1726.

MINISTRY OF FINANCE, TAIWAN (2003). Internet, http://www.dot.gov.tw/content1/num/edetail.asp?datafile=9111-12.txt Department of Taxation and Personal Inquiries by the Author, Taiwan, Taipei. 4.4. 2003.

MÖRSCH, M. (2002). Die Ökonomsichen Funktionen des Wettbewerbs im Gesundheitswesen: Anspruch, Realität und Wirtschaftspolitischer Handlungsbedarf, Gesundheitsökonomie und Qualitätsmanagement, Vol. 7, pp.155 - 160.

MORDUCH, J. (1995). Income Smoothing and Consumption Smoothing. Journal of Economic Perspectives, Vol. 9, pp. 103-114.

_____(1998). Does Microfinance Really Help the Poor? New Evidence from Flagship Programs in Bangladesh, Working Paper, Department of Economics and HIID, Harvard University.

_____(1999). The Micro-Finance Promise, Journal of Economic Literature, Vol. 37, No. 4, pp. 1569-1614.

_____(1999a). The Role of Subsidies in Microfinance: Evidence from the Grameen Bank, Journal of Development Economics, Vol. 60, pp. 229-248.

_____(2000). The Microfinance Schism, World Development, Vol. 28, No. 4, pp. 617-629.

MORGAN, J. (2000). Financing Public Goods by Means of Lotteries, Review of Economic Studies, Vol. 67, pp. 761 – 784.

MORGAN, J. AND SEFTON, M. (2000). Funding Public Goods with Lotteries: Experimental Evidence, Review of Economic Studies, Vol. 76, pp. 785 – 810.

MOSER, C. (1998). The Asset Vulnerability Framework: Reassessing Urban Poverty Reduction Strategies, World Development, Vol. 26, No. 1, pp. 1-19.

MUSAU, S. (1999). Community-Based Health Insurance: Experiences and Lessons Learned from East and Southern Africa, Technical Report No. 34, Partnership for Health Reform Project, Abt Associates, Bethesda, MD.

NABLI, M. AND NUGENT, J. (1989). The New Institutional Economics and its Applicability to Development, World Development, Vol. 17, No. 9, pp. 1333 – 1347.

NATIONAL STATISTIC HEALTH COORDINATION BOARD (2001). 1991-1999 Philippine Health Accounts, Manila.

NAVAJAS, S., SCHREINER, M., MEYER, R. L., GONZALES-VEGA, C. AND RODRIGUEZ-MEZA, J. (2000). Microcredit and the Poorest of the Poor: Theory and Evidence from Bolivia, World Development, Vol. 28, No. 2, pp. 333-346.

OLSON, M. (1969). The Logic of Collective Action: Public Goods and the Theory of Groups, New York.

OSTROM, E. (1998). A Behavioral Approach to the Rational Choice Theory of Collective Action, American Political Science Review, Vol.92, No.1, pp. 1-22.

PANNARUNOTHAI, S., SRITHAMRONGSAWAT, S., KONGPAN, M. AND THUMVANNA, P. (2000). Financing Reforms to the Thai Health Card Scheme, Health Policy and Planning, Vol. 15, No.3, pp. 303-311.

PREKER, A. S., CARRIN, G., DROR, D., JAKAB, M., HSIO, W. AND ARNHIN-TENKORANG, D. (2001). A Synthesis Report on the Role on Communities in Resource Mobilization and Risk Sharing, Commission on Macroeconomics and Health, Paper No. WG3:4.

PREKER , A. S. AND JAKAB, M. (2001). Role of Communities in Providing Financial Protection Against the Costs of Illness. In: Dror, D. and Preker, AS., Eds. Social Re-Insurance: Improved Risks Sharing for Low-Income and Excluded Groups. Washington: World Bank/ILO.

_____(2002). Effectiveness of Community Health Financing in Meeting the Costs of Illness, Bulletin of the World Health Organization, Vol. 80, No. 2, pp. 143-150.

PROVINCIAL PLANNING AND DEVELOPMENT OFFICE (2001). Discover Guimaras (leaflet), Jordan.

PROVINCIAL HEALTH OFFICE (2001), Unpublished Data, Jordan.

QUIGGING, J. (1991). On the Optimal Design of Lotteries. Econometrica, Vol. 58, pp. 1 – 16.

REARDON, T., FALL, A., KELLY, C., DELGADO, P., MATLON, J., HOPKINS, J. AND BADIANE, O. (1994). Is Income Diversification Agricultural-led in the West African Semi-Arid Tropics? In: Atsain, A.; Wangwe, S.; Drabek, A.G. (eds), Economic Policy Experience in Africa: What have we learned, IFPRI, Washington DC, pp. 207-230.

ROBINSON, M. AND WHITE, G. (1997). The Role of Civic Organization in the Provision of Social Services: Towards Synergy. Research for Action 37, World Institute for Development Economics Research (UNU/WIDER), Helsinki.

RON, A. (1999). NGOs in Community Health Insurance Schemes: Examples from Guatemala and the Philippines, Social Science and Medicine, Vol. 48, pp. 939-950.

ROSENZWEIG, M. (1988). Risk, Implicit Contracts and the Family in Rural Areas of Low-Income Countries, The Economic Journal, Vol. 98, pp. 1148 – 1170.

ROSENZWEIG, M. AND STARK, O. (1998). Consumption Smoothing, Migration, and Marriage: Evidence from Rural India, Journal of Political Economy, Vol. 97, No. 4, pp. 905 – 926.

SALAMON, L., AND ANHEIER, H. (1996). The Emerging Non-profit Sector. Manchester University Press, Manchester.

SALTMAN, R. B. (2002). Regulating Incentives: The Past and Present Role of the State in the Health Care System, Social Science and Medicine, Vol. 54, pp. 1677-1684.

SAMUELSON, P.A. (1954). The Pure Theory of Public Expenditure, Review of Economics and Statistics 36, pp. 387 – 389.

SCHIEBER, G. AND MAEDA, AKIKO (1999). Health Care Financing and Delivery in Developing Countries, Health Affairs, Vol. 18, No. 3, p. 193-205.

SEWA, http://www.sewa.org/insurance/products.htm, 16.05.2003.

SIEGEL, P., AND ALWANG, J. (1999). An Asset-Based Approach to Social Risk Management, SP Discussion Paper 9926, World Bank, Washington.

SIEGEL, P.; ALWANG, J. AND CANAGARAJAH, S. (2001). Viewing Microinsurance as a Social Risk Management Instrument, Social Protection Discussion Paper No. 116, The World Bank, Washington.

SONNEMANS, J., SCHRAM, A. AND OFFERMAN, T. (1999). Strategic Behavior in Public Good Games: When Partners Drift Apart, Economic Letters, Vol. 62, pp. 35-41.

STIERLE, F. (2000). Financing Health Care in Poor Countries – Issues and Lessons Learned, Gesellschaft für Technische Zusammenarbeit (GTZ), Eschborn.

SUPAKANKUNTI, S. (2000). Future Prospects of Voluntary Health Insurance in Thailand, in: Health Policy and Planning, Vol. 15, No. 1, p. 85-94.

_____(2001). Thailand: Determinants of Demand for Health Cards. Background Paper for the Working Group 3 of the Commission of Macroeconomics and Health, The World Bank, Washington, D.C.

UPPHOFF, N. (1993). Grassroots Organizations and NGOs in Rural Development: Opportunities with Diminishing States and Expanding Markets. World Development,Vol. 21, No. 4, pp. 607 – 622.

UNITED NATIONS DEVELOPMENT PROGRAM (2002). Human Development Report, New York, Oxford.

VON TROSCHKE, J. (1998). Gesundheits- und Krankheitsverhalten, in: Hurrelmann, K.; Laaser, U. eds., Handbuch der Gesundheitswissenschaften, Weinheim, München, pp. 371-394.

VAN TIL, J. (1987). The Three Sectors: Voluntarism in a Changing Political Economy. Journal of Voluntary Action Research, 16 (3), pp. 5 – 10.

WEBER, A. (2002). Health Care Financing in Guimaras, Unpublished report for the Gesellschaft für Technische Zusammenarbeit (GTZ), Eschborn.

_____(2002a). Insurance and Market Failure at the Microinsurance Level, in: Dror, D. and Preker, AS., Eds. Social Reinsurance: A New Approach to Sustainable Community Health Financing, World Bank/ILO, Washington, Geneva.

WEINBERGER, K. (2000). Women's Participation: An Economic Analysis in Rural Chad and Pakistan, Frankfurt am Main.

WENZEL, H. AND LAASER, U. (1990). Towards the Integrated Measurement of Quality of Life, in: Laaser, U.; Rocalla, E.J.; Rosenfeld, J.B.; Wenzel, H. eds., Costs and Benefits in Health Care and Prevention, Berlin, Heidelberg, New York, pp. 126 – 139.

WIESMAN, D. AND JÜTTING, J (2000),The Emerging Movement of Community-based Health Insurance in Sub-Saharan Africa: Experiences and Lessons Learned, Africa Spectrum, (2/2000), pp. 193-210.

WORLD BANK (2001). World Development Report 2000/2001, Washington.

WORLD BANK (2002). Ethiopia: Potential for Traditional Social Insurance for Supporting Health Care, IK Notes No. 48, Washington.

WORLD HEALTH ORGANIZATION (2003). Country Report Philippines, *Internet.* http://www.who.int/country/phl/en/, Geneva.

ZELLER, M. (1999). Towards Enhancing the Role of Microfinance for Safety Nets of the Poor, ZEF Discussion Paper on Development Policy No. 19, Center for Development Research, Bonn.

ZELLER, M., SCHRIEDER, G., VON BRAUN, J. AND HEIDHUES, F. (1997). Rural Finance for Food Security of the Poor: Implications for Research and Policy, Food Policy Review, No.4, Washington, D.C.: International Food Policy Research Institute (IFPRI).

Development Economics and Policy

Series edited by Franz Heidhues and Joachim von Braun

Band 1 Andrea Fadani: Agricultural Price Policy and Export and Food Production in Cameroon. A Farming Systems Analysis of Pricing Policies. The Case of Coffee-Based Farming Systems. 1999.

Band 2 Heike Michelsen: Auswirkungen der Währungsunion auf den Strukturanpassungsprozeß der Länder der afrikanischen Franc-Zone. 1995.

Band 3 Stephan Bea: Direktinvestitionen in Entwicklungsländern. Auswirkungen von Stabilisierungsmaßnahmen und Strukturreformen in Mexiko. 1995.

Band 4 Franz Heidhues / François Kamajou: Agricultural Policy Analysis – Proceedings of an International Seminar, held at the University of Dschang, Cameroon on May 26 and 27 1994, funded by the European Union under the Science and Technology Program (STD). 1996.

Band 5 Elke M. Förster: Protection or Liberalization? A Policy Analysis of the Korean Beef Sector. 1996.

Band 6 Gertrud Schrieder: The Role of Rural Finance for Food Security of the Poor in Cameroon. 1996.

Band 7 Nestor R. Ahoyo Adjovi: Economie des Systèmes de Production intégrant la Culture de Riz au Sud du Bénin: Potentialités, Contraintes et Perspectives. 1996.

Band 8 Jenny Müller: Income Distribution in the Agricultural Sector of Thailand. Empirical Analysis and Policy Options. 1996.

Band 9 Michael Brüntrup: Agricultural Price Policy and its Impact on Production, Income, Employment and the Adoption of Innovations. A Farming Systems Based Analysis of Cotton Policy in Northern Benin. 1997.

Band 10 Justin Bomda: Déterminants de l'Epargne et du Crédit, et leurs Implications pour le Développement du Système Financier Rural au Cameroun. 1998.

Band 11 John M. Msuya: Nutrition Improvement Projects in Tanzania: Implementation, Determinants of Performance, and Policy Implications. 1998.

Band 12 Andreas Neef: Auswirkungen von Bodenrechtswandel auf Ressourcennutzung und wirtschaftliches Verhalten von Kleinbauern in Niger und Benin. 1999.

Band 13 Susanna Wolf (ed.): The Future of EU-ACP Relations. 1999.

Band 14 Franz Heidhues / Gertrud Schrieder (eds.): Romania – Rural Finance in Transition Economies. 2000.

Band 15 Katinka Weinberger: Women's Participation. An Economic Analysis in Rural Chad and Pakistan. 2000.

Band 16 Christof Batzlen: Migration and Economic Development. Remittances and Investments in South Asia: A Case Study of Pakistan. 2000.

Band 17 Matin Qaim: Potential Impacts of Crop Biotechnology in Developing Countries. 2000.

Band 18 Jean Senahoun: Programmes d'ajustement structurel, sécurité alimentaire et durabilité agricole. Une approche d'analyse intégrée, appliquée au Bénin. 2001.

Band 19 Torsten Feldbrügge: Economics of Emergency Relief Management in Developing Countries. With Case Studies on Food Relief in Angola and Mozambique. 2001.

Band 20 Claudia Ringler: Optimal Allocation and Use of Water Resources in the Mekong River Basin: Multi-Country and Intersectoral Analyses. 2001.

Band 21   Arnim Kuhn: Handelskosten und regionale (Des-)Integration. Russlands Agrarmärkte in der Transformation. 2001.

Band 22   Ortrun Anne Gronski: Stock Markets and Economic Growth. Evidence from South Africa. 2001.

Band 23   Patrick Webb / Katinka Weinberger (eds.): Women Farmers. Enhancing Rights, Recognition and Productivity. 2001.

Band 24   Mingzhi Sheng: Lebensmittelkonsum und -konsumtrends in China. Eine empirische Analyse auf der Basis ökonometrischer Nachfragemodelle. 2002.

Band 25   Maria Iskandarani: Economics of Household Water Security in Jordan. 2002.

Band 26   Romeo Bertolini: Telecommunication Services in Sub-Saharan Africa. An Analysis of Access and Use in the Southern Volta Region in Ghana. 2002.

Band 27   Dietrich Müller-Falcke: Use and Impact of Information and Communication Technologies in Developing Countries' Small Businesses. Evidence from Indian Small Scale Industry. 2002.

Band 28   Wolfram Erhardt: Financial Markets for Small Enterprises in Urban and Rural Northern Thailand. Empirical Analysis on the Demand for and Supply of Financial Services, with Particular Emphasis on the Determinants of Credit Access and Borrower Transaction Costs. 2002.

Band 29   Wensheng Wang: The Impact of Information and Communication Technologies on Farm Households in China. 2002.

Band 30   Shyamal K. Chowdhury: Institutional and Welfare Aspects of the Provision and Use of Information and Communication Technologies in the Rural Areas of Bangladesh and Peru. 2002.

Band 31   Annette Luibrand: Transition in Vietnam. Impact of the Rural Reform Process on an Ethnic Minority. 2002.

Band 32   Felix Ankomah Asante: Economic Analysis of Decentralisation in Rural Ghana. 2003.

Band 33   Chodechai Suwanaporn: Determinants of Bank Lending in Thailand: An Empirical Examination for the Years 1992 to 1996. 2003.

Band 34   Abay Asfaw: Costs of Illness, Demand for Medical Care, and the Prospect of Community Health Insurance Schemes in the Rural Areas of Ethiopia. 2003.

Band 35   Gi-Soon Song: The Impact of Information and Communication Technologies (ICTs) on Rural Households. A Holistic Approach Applied to the Case of Lao People's Democratic Republic. 2003.

Band 36   Daniela Lohlein: An Economic Analysis of Public Good Provision in Rural Russia. The Case of Education and Health Care. 2003.

Band 37   Johannes Woelcke. Bio-Economics of Sustainable Land Management in Uganda. 2003.

Band 38   Susanne M. Ziemek: The Economics of Volunteer Labor Supply. An Application to Countries of a Different Development Level. 2003.

Band 39   Doris Wiesmann: An International Nutrition Index. Concept and Analyses of Food Insecurity and Undernutrition at Country Levels. 2004.

Band 40   Isaac Osei-Akoto: The Economics of Rural Health Insurance. The Effects of Formal and Informal Risk-Sharing Shemes in Ghana. 2004.

Band 41   Yuansheng Jiang: Health Insurance Demand and Health Risk Management in Rural China. 2004.

Band 42   Roukayatou Zimmermann: Biotechnology and Value-added Traits inFood Crops: Rele-
          vance for Developing Countries and Economic Analyses. 2004.

Band 43   F. Markus Kaiser: Incentives in Community-based Health Insurance Schemes. 2004.

www.peterlang.de